About Island Press

Since 1984, the nonprofit organization Island Press has been stimulating, shaping, and communicating ideas that are essential for solving environmental problems worldwide. With more than 1,000 titles in print and some 30 new releases each year, we are the nation's leading publisher on environmental issues. We identify innovative thinkers and emerging trends in the environmental field. We work with world-renowned experts and authors to develop cross-disciplinary solutions to environmental challenges.

Island Press designs and executes educational campaigns, in conjunction with our authors, to communicate their critical messages in print, in person, and online using the latest technologies, innovative programs, and the media. Our goal is to reach targeted audiences—scientists, policy makers, environmental advocates, urban planners, the media, and concerned citizens—with information that can be used to create the framework for long-term ecological health and human well-being.

Island Press gratefully acknowledges major support from The Bobolink Foundation, Caldera Foundation, The Curtis and Edith Munson Foundation, The Forrest C. and Frances H. Lattner Foundation, The JPB Foundation, The Kresge Foundation, The Summit Charitable Foundation, Inc., and many other generous organizations and individuals.

The opinions expressed in this book are those of the author(s) and do not necessarily reflect the views of our supporters.

Praise for

Arrested Mobility: Overcoming the Threat to Black Movement

"Charles Brown has shaped the national discourse over equity in transportation, the use of open space, and physical activity for cohorts of public health practitioners across the nation. Here, he brings together his insights on these issues to highlight the numerous ways in which structural racism is woven into the fabric of the American landscape. Arrested mobility has profound impacts on the experiences of people of color and in particular, Black Americans. Brown helps us understand that only by dismantling the internal structures of thought that stigmatize and dehumanize Black lives, the structures of political power that perpetuate social and physical immobility, and the decades of decision making that have manifested a physical landscape that arrests Black mobility can true social, economic, and health justice be achieved."

— Gabriel E. Kaplan, Assistant Director of Health Services, Sonoma County

"How do we first recognize, then *un-arrest* the mobility of Black and other marginalized people as they move through communities, spaces, and places? This timely, creative, and thoroughly engaging book offers workable policy and planning frameworks of mobility justice and racial justice to professionals, advocates, and others responsible for shaping our collective futures."

—Julian Agyeman, Professor of Urban and Environmental Policy and Planning, Tufts University

"More than ever, this book is needed. A must-read for people in power, as well as advocates, and anyone who cares about people and cities. Charles has experience and knowledge, explains clearly the problems, and provides solutions. Clearly, we can create equitable cities, but actions like those he suggests must be implemented. Now."

—Gil Penalosa, Founder and Chair, 8 80 Cities and Cities for Everyone

ARRESTED MOBILITY

Overcoming the Threat to Black Movement

CHARLES T. BROWN

Washington | Covelo

© 2025, Charles T. Brown

All rights reserved under International and Pan-American Copyright Conventions. No part of this book may be reproduced in any form or by any means without permission in writing from the publisher: Island Press, 2000 M Street, NW, Suite 480-B, Washington, DC 20036-3319.

Library of Congress Control Number: 2024950094

All Island Press books are printed on environmentally responsible materials.

Manufactured in the United States of America
10 9 8 7 6 5 4 3 2 1

KEYWORDS: biking while Black, community resilience, design justice, driving while Black, environmental design, individual racism, institutional racism, interpersonal racism, land use regulations, overpolicing, physical mobility, policing, racial discrimination, redlining, scooting while Black, segregation, social mobility, structural racism, The Talk, traffic safety, urban planning, urban renewal, walking while Black, White supremacy

TO MY LOVELY WIFE, LATASKA:
God couldn't have granted me a better partner to spend this lifetime with.
Your unwavering love and sacrifices are the foundation upon which
all my dreams are built. I am forever grateful.

TO MY MOTHER, DEBRA:
My hero, whose strength and wisdom have shaped me into
who I am today. This is as much yours as it is mine.

TO MY CHILDREN, CHRISTIAN, LAYLA, AND CAMDYN:
You are the light of my life, and everything I do is for your future.
Your love gives me purpose, and I would give my life
to protect and uplift you.

CONTENTS

Foreword by Stephanie Gidigbi Jenkins | xi
Preface | xv
Acknowledgments | xix

Introduction | 1

ONE   How Arrested Mobility Is Created Through Polity and Policy | 13

TWO   The Urban Planning Strategies That Have Shaped Our Communities | 29

THREE   Policing: The Means by Which Unequal Systems Are Reinforced | 55

FOUR   Un-Arresting Mobility: What It Will Take to Solve Inequity in Mobility | 69

FIVE   Arrested Mobility Solutions in Action | 91

Conclusion: Breaking the Silence | 117

Notes | 123
Bibliography | 151
About the Author | 173

FOREWORD

By Stephanie Gidigbi Jenkins

> *"To be free is not merely to cast off one's chains, but to live in a way that respects and enhances the freedom of others."*
>
> —Nelson Mandela

Imagine being awakened by a morning chorus of birds and early risers stirring outside your window. You turn to feel the warmth of the sun on your skin. Your mind and body are conflicted about accepting the invitation to start a new day. Another dream lingers in your spirit, trading places with the promise of possibility that a new day brings: the power and privilege of choice.

It's hard to imagine that the decisions you make throughout the day are partly predefined by where you live, your racial ethnicity defined by social stereotypes and the cumulative impacts of past and current government policies. The summation of this truth is defined by the term *arrested mobility*, coined by professor Charles T. Brown, founder and CEO of Equitable Cities.

Charles and I met while speaking on a transportation and access panel years ago, but his work as a pracademic (an academic practitioner in the field of urban planning, serving at the time as a senior researcher with the Alan M. Voorhees Transportation Center at Rutgers University) preceded our interaction. We later served on the Advisory Committee for Transportation Equity for the US Department of Transportation. He remains one of the foremost thought leaders, whose insight I deeply respect.

He's a native son of the rural South, husband, father, and believer in the possibility of systemic change.

Born in the small country town of Shuqualak in Noxubee County, Mississippi, Charles grew up just a few counties away from where President Reagan launched his "let's make America great again" general election campaign in 1980 at the Neshoba County Fair, within walking distance of Philadelphia, Mississippi, where civil rights activists were killed in what are known as the Freedom Summer murders. President Reagan, who was a masterful communicator, often used dogwhistle language to garner support without provoking opposition. His speech in support of "states' rights" sought to appeal to White voters who resented civil rights efforts of the 1960s and 1970s, targeting policies that redressed historic patterns of racial discrimination. He rose to power as governor of California, where he denounced housing and civil rights law and popularized the derogatory reference to Black single mothers as "Welfare Queens" while failing to recognize the poverty trap of racism. The parallelism between Reagan and Trump is uncanny, yet it is an opportunity to learn from history in creating the future we seek.

When Charles invited me to write this foreword, I found myself reflecting on the tale of two realities associated with the American Dream and the implication of arrested mobility tied to race and class.

The American Dream is the fundamental belief that if one works hard, secures a good education, and maintains a level of respectability, anything is possible. The emphasis on individual effort ignores the structural barriers that limit mobility. Any solution will need to incorporate a systemic response to the challenge.

For Black people in the United States, any pursuit of the American Dream can quickly become a nightmare that they may never wake up from, as was the case for Breonna Taylor. The reality is that Black women in Washington, DC, account for about half of all births and yet 90% of pregnancy-related deaths.[1] According to *The New York Times*, between 2016 and 2021 police killed more than 400 unarmed drivers or passengers, at a rate of more than one killing per week of unarmed motorists, who were disproportionately Black.[2] As a Black mother of Black children I find the work personal; as a wife of a Black spouse I pray I never get the call.

It's concerning because there seems to be no safe way to move as a Black person in America, whether you are a Harvard professor trying to enter your own home, like Henry Louis Gates, or an avid bird watcher simply enjoying nature, like Christian Cooper. However, arrested mobility isn't just about the racial profiling experience of Black people; the term encapsulates the social, economic, political, and cultural ills of racism.

It reflects centuries of enforced subjugation through a racialized caste system embedded in the founding doctrine of the United States, intertwined in the social norms of American life.

Arrested mobility personifies the racialized violence and overpolicing of Black bodies that shocked our collective consciousness after the death of George Floyd during the pandemic of 2020. This helped to crystallize for the larger public the plight of Black people, who have felt the weight of their race on their necks for over 400 years, when the first documented enslaved Africans arrived on American soil in 1619.

It wasn't until I found myself standing at the "door of no return" in the Cape Coast Castle of Ghana with my husband, a descendant of enslaved people in the United States and fourth-generation resident of Washington, DC, that I could truly grasp the sobering reality of the transatlantic slave trade, the postcolonial impact of slavery on Black people in the Americas and on the continent of Africa. We grappled with the legacy of slavery and fortitude of his ancestors and all Black Americans who endured the Middle Passage, slavery, the Jim Crow laws that enforced racial segregation, and post–Civil Rights movement realities wherein race still affects Black life. We discussed how neocolonial rule has created cycles of dependency, political instability, and economic challenges, causing the migration of Black people to seek refuge abroad.

It should be noted that most immigrants to the United States and their descendants tend to make significant economic gains but overlook the systemic factors that influence their success and limit others.[3] The US federal government has historically granted economic advantages to White Americans while systematically excluding people of color. For example, the Homestead Act of 1862 provided free or low-cost land to 1.5 million White families while failing to honor its promise of providing "40 acres and a mule" during Reconstruction to the forebears of enslaved people.

Redlining and discriminatory housing practices have created generational havoc and locked in the impact of segregated neighborhoods, where communities of color often have less access to high-quality schools and jobs, limiting their economic prospects.

Coupled with the implications of climate change, many formerly redlined areas create sacrifice zones with low-lying homes, limited tree cover, and more pavement, which reduces rain absorption and increases erosion from stormwater. These areas often have outdated infrastructure that can't manage severe rainfall, leading to flooding. Additionally, they receive less investment in environmental resources such as trees, parks, and drainage systems, leaving them less financially equipped to prepare for and recover from natural disasters. Charles documents throughout this book the cumulative impact of social, economic, environmental, and cultural factors that lead to arrested mobility.

In the wake of the Supreme Court decision on affirmative action, new solutions must be developed to address the root causes of the challenges outlined by Charles in each chapter of this book. I recognize this book as a labor of love, so I hope you enjoy it as much as I have. May we answer the call to ensure we all get and stay free.

PREFACE

I was reared by an amazing, beautiful Black woman in the loving, predominantly Black town of Shuqualak, Mississippi. Shuqualak, nestled in Noxubee County, is a place where history runs deep, marked by the governor of Mississippi seeking refuge in the county during the Civil War and Macon bearing witness to the White supremacist terrorism of the Red Summer of 1919. These events are part of a larger narrative that has shaped the lives of Black people in Noxubee County, but they are not the whole story. This land is also a testament to the resilience and strength of a community that, despite the odds, continues to thrive.

My journey in Shuqualak was shaped by the intersection of personal and systemic challenges. Despite the unwavering love and support from my family, neighbors, and the residents of this close-knit community, I couldn't escape the painful realities that surrounded me. My father, a brilliant and talented man, was visibly present in my life yet tragically inaccessible because of his struggle with drug addiction, a battle that ultimately took his life and with it the hero I longed for in a father. His struggle is emblematic of the broader challenges that have arrested the mobility of so many in our community—a reflection of how public policy, planning decisions, and policing practices have created environments where potential is stifled and lives are often cut short.

In Shuqualak and across Noxubee County, the high poverty rates, low educational attainment, and limited access to healthcare are not just statistics; they are the direct results of historical and ongoing policies that have systematically disadvantaged Black communities. The legacy of segregation, the lack of resources for public schools, and the planning decisions that have isolated our communities from economic opportunities are all part of a broader strategy that has kept Black people from moving forward. These are not just accidental outcomes; they are the deliberate results of public policies and planning decisions designed to maintain racial hierarchies.

The roots of these challenges are deeply embedded in the fabric of our society, reflected in the overpolicing of our communities, the exclusionary practices in public policy, the inequitable distribution of resources, and the planning decisions that have consistently prioritized the needs of others over our own. One of the most glaring examples of this is the way school integration was systematically undermined through White flight and the establishment of segregation academies in Noxubee County. These institutions were not just about education; they were about preserving power and control, about ensuring that the resources and opportunities that should have been available to all were kept within the hands of a few.

The economic and social impacts of these actions were devastating. The disinvestment in public education, combined with the broader decline of the local economy, left Noxubee County struggling with high poverty rates and low educational attainment. Even today, the county faces significant challenges, including a lack of access to essential infrastructure such as broadband internet, which further hinders opportunities for advancement. However, it's essential to recognize that Noxubee County is also a place of deep-rooted community spirit, where people come together in times of need and where a strong sense of identity and pride prevails. This resilience is a testament to the strength of the people who live there and their determination to create a better future, despite the systemic barriers they face.

Generally speaking, the barriers Black people face are not just external; they have also been internalized, creating a cycle where the community unconsciously reinforces the very structures that hold it back. Police misconduct in our neighborhoods has fostered a sense of distrust not just toward law enforcement but toward each other, weakening the bonds that could unite us in challenging the status quo. The normalization of discriminatory policies and planning practices has led to a resignation that change is impossible—a mindset that further cements the status quo and perpetuates the cycle of arrested mobility.

The mental health toll of living in such an environment is palpable. Chronic stress, anxiety, and a sense of hopelessness permeate the community, making it even harder for people to take risks, seek new opportunities, or advocate for change. This emotional burden is compounded by the physical realities of police misconduct, inadequate public policy, and exclusionary planning practices that have left our communities struggling with a low quality of life, as reflected in the statistics I mentioned earlier.

In Shuqualak and Noxubee County, the legacy of police misconduct, exclusionary public policy, and inequitable planning practices has been a significant barrier, compounding the external forces of discrimination that have long kept Black people from moving forward. But recognizing this reality is the first step toward breaking the cycle and unlocking the true potential of this resilient community and others like it. The history we carry is heavy, but it also serves as a reminder of the work that still needs to be done and the possibilities that await when we confront and dismantle the barriers to our mobility.

Surprisingly, I didn't often experience blatant interpersonal racism as a child or young adult in Mississippi, a state often considered the birthplace of racism in America. However, I became acutely aware of it through my early readings of *The Autobiography of Malcolm X* and the tragic stories of Emmett Till and Medgar Evers and the brutal violence faced by Fannie Lou Hamer, whose words delivered in a 1964 speech at the Williams Institutional CME Church in Harlem, New York, "I am sick and tired of being sick and tired," still echo today.

Learning about the 1964 murders of three voter registration volunteers for the Congress of Racial Equality, James Chaney, Andrew Goodman, and Michael Schwerner, just forty-five minutes away from my hometown of Shuqualak, and knowing that Jackson, Mississippi, and Money, Mississippi, were only a couple of hours away, showed me how close to home deep racial inequality and violence actually were. I have family members from the Mississippi Delta, and although I did not encounter interpersonal racism directly in my youth, it loomed over our lives through these painful narratives.

My personal experiences with interpersonal racism began later in life—in college, during my military service, and as I pursued and excelled in the urban planning field. This is an important fact because although I had moved away from Mississippi, where violence against Black people was arguably a daily occurrence during the Civil Rights movement, I felt interpersonal racism most deeply in places and communities that were seen to be safer and less discriminatory toward Black people.

I never experienced physical violence, but I often faced bias, discriminatory behaviors, microaggressions, and attempts at social exclusion—although my social network was too broad for those to be fully effective. I vividly remember instances in corporate settings where White women would refuse to get on elevators with me alone, or if they did, they would clutch their purses tightly. I wasn't perceived as credible on professional topics without White validation, unlike my White male peers, who were automatically granted credibility despite having the same education and experience.

In graduate school, a professor expressed surprise when he learned I was from Noxubee County, Mississippi. He had visited the area "back in the day" and had apparently never met a Black person from there who could read. His astonished question to me was, "How did you get here?" Even in professional environments, I encountered situations where my White colleagues, who were technically my staff, were presumed to be the managers during site visits or community outreach sessions.

One particularly striking experience happened in Metuchen, New Jersey, a predominantly White area, where I was leading a small team of student researchers as the principal investigator on a study of pedestrian safety at bus stops. Despite the obvious nature of our work—conducting direct observations in the field in a known high-traffic area—local police were called, responding to a report that we were "stalking" residents. Although my team consisted of White students, it was me, the Black leader, who was asked to provide identification and evidence of the study. Fortunately, I had my Rutgers ID and a letter from the supporting agency on hand. This experience stood in stark contrast to a similar observation study in Camden, New Jersey, a majority minority city, where residents approached us with water and chairs to help us endure the sweltering heat, even though my all-White team was initially hesitant to go there.

These experiences highlight the stark and often unspoken realities of interpersonal racism—a reality that is all too familiar, regardless of where one might be.

I think of these experiences in my work. I bring my own lived experience to the perspective I have. But I also recognize that what I've been able to achieve makes me privileged compared to a lot of Black people in America today. Therefore, I see it as a responsibility to help move our country forward to address the root causes that have arrested the social and physical mobility of Black people everywhere.

It is through this lens that I bring you into this work of arrested mobility, focusing on how policing, public policy, polity, and planning have conspired to hold back communities such as Shuqualak, Noxubee County, Mississippi, and so many others across the nation. But it's also through this lens that I see the potential for change, rooted in the resilience, strength, and unwavering spirit of our people.

ACKNOWLEDGMENTS

First and foremost, I give my utmost thanks to my Lord and Savior Jesus Christ. Since childhood, I've carried with me the Bible verse, "The Spirit of the Lord is upon me" (Luke 4:18), which has guided and strengthened me through every challenge.

To my lovely wife, LaTaska, and our children, Christian, Layla, and Camdyn: Your love, sacrifice, and unwavering support have been the bedrock of my life. None of this would be possible without you. It is my greatest honor to serve you as husband, father, protector, and provider.

To my mother, Debra Cotton, my father, Willie C. McNeese (Rest in Peace), my brothers, Louis Cotton and Tyrone McNeese, and my sisters, LaTonya Taylor and LaTika Brown: I love you unconditionally and hope that I've made you proud.

To my uncle Joe Dancy Sr. (Rest in Peace) and my aunt Mable Dancy, and my cousins Joe Dancy Jr. and Jabreka Dancy: Thank you for being a steadfast source of love, guidance, and support throughout my life.

To my in-laws, Eddie McGee, Exelena McGee, and Verinda Waters, as well as the rest of the family I've been blessed to know for over two decades: Thank you for your steadfast support and for always being there for us. Your presence in our lives is a true blessing.

I also want to honor my elementary school teachers, Nancy Bell and Bobby Jean Moody, who poured into me like second mothers. Rest in peace and power to both of you. You truly loved me, stayed in touch until the end, and guided me through pivotal moments in my life, from college to fatherhood. Mrs. Moody's magical jellybeans had me believing that anything was possible.

A special thank you to Tiffany Young and Robyn Taylor, two incredible Black women who spent countless nights with me discussing the essence of arrested mobility and even personally invested in my first project on the topic. Your belief in me has meant the world.

I am deeply grateful to my publisher, Island Press, and my editor, Heather Boyer, for your keen insights and tireless efforts in shaping this book. Your expertise has been invaluable. A special thank you to Elizabeth Doerr, who helped mold my thoughts and ideas into these pages and walked with me throughout this journey.

To my circle of family, friends, associates, and confidants who have inspired, encouraged, and supported me both personally and professionally over the years: Thank you for always being in my corner. While I can't name everyone, special thanks go to Alonzo Williams, Adam Walosik, Adrian Rogers, Barbara McNeese, Dr. Devajyoti Deka, Christian Duncan, Christina Hill, Glenn Robinson Sr., Dr. Larnie Booker, Veronica Davis, tamika l. butler, Randall "Keith" Benjamin II, Dr. Melicent Miller, Salento Boddie, Johari Powell, and Henry Brown. Your impact on my life is beyond measure. I am forever indebted to you.

To my fraternity brothers of Kappa Alpha Psi Fraternity, Inc., particularly the Winter Park (Florida) Alumni Chapter and the New Brunswick (New Jersey) Alumni Chapter: Thank you for your unwavering brotherhood and support. I am also deeply grateful to my fellow soldiers in the US military for your service and camaraderie.

Thanks to the many researchers, podcast producers, writers, and editors who contribute to the Arrested Mobility Podcast and report. Your hard work and dedication help bring these critical stories to light.

Finally, to my hometown of Shuqualak, Mississippi, and all the people of Noxubee County, Mississippi: I am because WE are. Go Tigers!

Introduction

"Birds born in a cage think flying is an illness."
—Alejandro Jodorowsky

When I give presentations around the world on the importance of centering equity in transportation, I start with racial segregation maps. They're useful in showing the stark racial and ethnic divisions in cities across the United States and illustrating how past transportation and land use decisions shape present-day mobility challenges.

The maps are color coded to show the predominant race in each neighborhood (White indicated by blue, Black by green, Hispanic by orange, and Asian by peach). There is rarely a spot where the green, orange, and peach neighborhoods seep into the blue ones. "Every city in America looks something like this," I say, pointing to maps of Peoria, Illinois; Detroit, Michigan; Houston, Texas; Atlanta, Georgia; and Washington, DC.

Without fail, someone asks, "Are there any exceptions to these cities?" Jokingly, I respond by showing a map of Portland, Oregon, and exclaiming, "Yes, go to Portland, where there are no Black people!" That line usually gets a laugh from everyone, even people from Portland. But the truth behind it is far from funny. The maps reveal deep segregation, born from a history of exclusion, that still dictates who has the freedom to move, to live, and to thrive in the city today.

Portland—and Oregon as a whole—were built on exclusion. The state of Oregon was founded on a Black Exclusion Law, which was enshrined in its 1857 constitution and prohibited Black people from settling in the state.[1] Although the law has been repealed, its legacy is alive and well. Portland remains the Whitest big city in America, with more than 66 percent of its residents identifying as White.[2] And for the few Black people who settled in Oregon—primarily drawn by the shipbuilding industry during World War II—racism limited their opportunities. As in other cities around the country, Black residents were systematically excluded from wealth-building opportunities, redlined into certain neighborhoods, denied mortgages, and later displaced by highway expansions and urban renewal projects that bulldozed their communities.

Oregon's political leaders have been slow to address the systemic racism in the state. Laws and policies designed to promote racial equity are often weakly enforced or underfunded, and racial disparities in public infrastructure persist. Even in Portland, which has a reputation for being progressive, policing has been weaponized against Black bodies in public spaces. Portland has the fifth highest arrest disparity rate in the country where Black Portlanders are arrested at a rate 4.3 times higher than White people and are killed by police 3.9 times more often than White people.[3] Existing in public as a Black person comes with inherent risks, from police or civilians.

In Portland in 2017, a White supremacist fatally stabbed two men and injured a third, all who were intervening while the man hurled racist and anti-Muslim slurs at two Black teenagers on a MAX Light Rail train.[4]

In September 2023 Adrian Cummins stabbed two Black teenagers on a MAX train in Portland.[5] The teens were attacked without provocation, with one suffering a life-threatening injury that necessitated emergency surgery.

Incidents like these call attention to the lack of safety for people of color moving about the community. This is arrested mobility. The ability to move freely, safely, and confidently through one's city—whether in a car, on foot, by bike, by e-scooter, or by public transit—is a fundamental aspect of participating in society. Yet for Black and Brown people, mobility is constrained by systemic racism in policing, planning, polity, and policy. They are more likely to live in neighborhoods with dangerous roads and less likely to benefit from the city's vaunted bike infrastructure. Their access to safe public transit is often undermined by racial profiling and violence.

Although Portland is celebrated for its investment in public transit, bike lanes, and sustainable urban development, these improvements often came at a cost to communities of color. Many Black and Brown residents were pushed out of their neighborhoods as property values rose in areas that received transit investments, forcing them into more isolated, less connected parts of the city with higher crash rates and fewer public amenities.[6,7] Therefore, Portland's investments in green infrastructure may have created a reputation for progressiveness, but they also reinforced the racial divide.

I saw this in my research for a 2021 study for PeopleForBikes, "Where Do We Go From Here? Breaking Down Barriers to Biking in the U.S."[8] Although Portland boasts one of the highest bike ridership rates in the country, our study found that Black and Brown residents rarely felt comfortable or safe using the city's bike infrastructure. During a focus group with Black Muslim residents, the consensus was clear: They did not feel that Portland's bike culture was meant for them. The city's bike lanes may be celebrated by White cyclists, but Black and Brown residents felt alienated, excluded, and in some cases even targeted. Hijab-wearing women in the group reported feeling specifically vulnerable while cycling, adding yet another layer of racial and cultural exclusion.[9]

But Portland also offers a glimmer of hope. There are efforts under way to un-arrest mobility. The city's BIKETOWN program, launched in 2016 in partnership with Nike, was designed with equity in mind.[10] In fact, BIKETOWN was one of the few bike share programs in the country to prioritize station placement in low-income neighborhoods.[11,12] Of the ten bike share systems we looked at in various US cities, BIKETOWN was the only one that had a higher-than-average station density in socioeconomically disadvantaged neighborhoods and lower density in the advantaged neighborhoods.[13] It was the highest-ranking program for bike share equity among the ten cities.[14,15]

Even in a city as overwhelmingly White as Portland, planners and policymakers can—and must—take steps to un-arrest mobility for Black and Brown people. The stakes are high. For Black people, the right to move freely isn't just a matter of convenience or comfort. It's a matter of life and death.

BEING BLACK IN PUBLIC

Talk with any Black person in America and they can recount an interaction with law enforcement. When asked, I can immediately recall three such incidents, all of which took place in a car. Once in college, the car in which I was a passenger with three other Black men was pulled over for what seemed to be no reason. Another time as a passenger with a White woman driving, the officer pulled us over and asked my White companion whether she was okay, as if *I* were the one speeding. The third time was when I was driving, and the officer asked my wife whether she was okay.

Although I was not physically harmed on these occasions, the feeling of dread, the question about whether this was the moment that I become the next name added to the rolls of Black men shot by police, entered my brain.

As a Black man in America, I expect these encounters every time I leave the house. I make mental calculations when I'm choosing my clothes. If I'm wearing a hoodie, particularly a black or dark-colored one, will I be targeted? If I run through a predominantly White neighborhood, will someone find me suspicious? Will wearing a suit be enough to make people less suspicious of me?

When a person has to make these mental calculations about safety and security and is not able to move freely through a city, that person's mobility is arrested. What I experience day to day is what most if not all Black people in America experience. Of course, many people who are historically marginalized, including Native American and Latinx people, women, people with disabilities, and gender nonconforming people, all experience a lack of safety in public to some degree, but for the purpose of this book, I'm focusing on the experience of Black Americans. This is my lived experience and the experience of most Black Americans, as well as the focus of my research and work. The circumstances may differ from person to person, and my more recent relative economic privilege might shield me from *some* dangerous scenarios, but for all of us Black Americans, the danger looms constantly—consciously or not.

For all intents and purposes, I'm a successful person. I am a veteran of the US armed forces. I have an advanced degree. I am a professor. I am a CEO. Yet still, I feel the effects of my limited mobility because racism is in the air we breathe.

Beverly Daniel Tatum, expert on the psychology of racism, calls racism a "smog" in her seminal book *Why Are All the Black Kids Sitting Together in the Cafeteria?*[16] "Cultural racism—the cultural images and messages that affirm the assumed superiority of Whites and the assumed inferiority of people of color—is like smog in the air," she writes. "Some days it is so thick it is visible, other times it is less apparent, but always, day in and day out, we are breathing it in."[17]

This smog hinders the movement of Black Americans, whether it is from gaining upward mobility or moving around public spaces in a society built for people who don't look like us. I refer to this as arrested mobility.

I also think of arrested mobility like a cancer. If you ignore it long enough, it can kill you. This book and the work I do are dedicated to fighting that cancer every day.

Arrested mobility, I argue, is the direct manifestation of structural racism (racism that is personal, interpersonal, institutional, and cultural), which has led to the intentional and deliberate overpolicing of Black Americans. It has led to disinvestment in Black communities and communities of color that has cut them off from generational wealth development as well as everything that is afforded a person to achieve the so-called American Dream.

For the arrest of physical mobility, we need to look at the various types of violence against Black Americans. Some of it is more direct, such as police killing and brutality in predominantly Black communities, and some more subtle forms of violence that come from living in a place where the streets are not safe.

A 2022 study by Matthew A. Raifman and Ernani F. Choma from Boston University's School of Public Health and Harvard's T.H. Chan School of Public Health, respectively, found that Black Americans had the highest mortality rate per mile of travel by means of walking, bicycling, or light-duty vehicles (e.g., passenger cars).[18] The rates were especially high for cycling: Black cyclists were 4.5 times more likely to die in an accident than White cyclists, 2.2 times more likely than White pedestrians, and 1.8 times more likely than White people in vehicles.[19]

This inequity is rooted in power: who has power, who maintains power, and the social forces that lead to such power, which is strongly linked to race. This seems to be changing on the surface in terms of who is in power, but there are still two parallel systems of opportunity: one for White people and one for everyone else.

Avant-garde filmmaker Alejandro Jodorowsky gave us the oft-quoted words, "Birds born in a cage think flying is an illness." I feel this deeply when I think about arrested mobility. It is as if we are caged birds when our movement is limited by the barriers created by a society designed from the outset to oppress us. We have internalized the historic oppression by limiting our freedoms for our own safety. We have seen what has happened to Black Americans who are perceived as a threat. We have been in situations where we have been perceived as a threat. And we have been given less access to the means of social mobility. We move about the world as if movement were an illness.

Yet Black people have always resisted. Since the time of enslavement, Black people have worked for racial justice. We have known our rights. Yet here we are in the twenty-first century still fighting for the most basic right to move around our communities freely and to have equitable access to transportation, jobs, housing, parks and open spaces, and basic services.

Certainly, much has improved, but as we see year after year, police kill disproportionately more Black people than people of all other races. Between 24 and 27 percent of people killed by police in the United States between 2018 and 2023 were Black when only 13 percent of the population is Black. This is all despite the fact that Black people are more likely to be unarmed and less likely to be threatening someone at the time they were killed.[20] Thus, much work remains.

Mobility embodies freedom and allows people, places, and cities to thrive. Moreover, in the United States, freedom—synonymous with national identity—is often represented by acts of movement such as driving a car, riding a bicycle, walking down the street, or traveling to a different city. However, for Black Americans, exercising freedom of mobility has always meant confronting the harsh reality of White fear, fragility, and violence.

WHAT IS MOBILITY?

On a personal level, mobility is the ability to move one's body freely and the freedom to move around any given space. *Social mobility* implies a metaphorical upward movement, an ability to participate freely in our economic institutions and thus to build personal wealth in order to live a happy, healthy, and stress-free life. There are several indicators of lower rates of social mobility among Black Americans, including higher Black unemployment rates (between June 2023 and June 2024, Black unemployment remained between 5.6 and 6.3 percent, whereas White unemployment fluctuated between 3.1 and 3.5 percent[21]) and lower high school graduation rates for Black students (for the 2021–2022 school year, 81 percent of Black students and 90 percent of White students graduated[22]).

Physical mobility and social mobility are intrinsically linked. Both forms of mobility play a fundamental role in the lives of urban, suburban, and rural residents. In order to access the levers of economic and social mobility, we must be able to move safely and freely around our communities to access jobs, to participate in civic engagement, to socialize with friends and family, and to engage in leisure activities.

In an ideal world, physical mobility would be accessible to every single person equitably.

WHAT IS ARRESTED MOBILITY?

I use the term *arrested mobility* to mean a condition that is imposed only on people of a certain race, specifically Black people. Arrested mobility is the intentional and incomplete access to all means of movement in public and sometimes private spaces by way of deliberate overpolicing, which has, in turn, made us less safe and limited social mobility. Arrested mobility leads to paralysis among Black Americans who find themselves trapped in a system that confines their physical movements and provides only narrow, perilous openings for social mobility. Arrested mobility makes it difficult for Black people to engage in civil society.

Although arrested mobility is most acute among foundational Black Americans who are descended from enslaved Africans, it applies to all marginalized people and is compounded with each layer of marginalization: all people of color, low-income people, people with disabilities, and female, queer, trans, elderly, and unhoused people.

With each layer of marginalization, the conditions are incrementally more difficult. For example, disabled Black Americans face profound difficulties not just in getting around a city but also in accessing healthcare. And Black trans women are the most at risk of homicide among the already highly vulnerable trans community.[23]

Because of the legacy of structural racism, White supremacy, povertyism, and ableism, we do not live in a society where mobility is afforded in the same way to everyone. People with physical or mental disabilities are forced to adapt to a world built for the able-bodied. The lack of infrastructure for modes of travel other than the car and disinvestment in public transit in low-income neighborhoods make getting around vastly more difficult for people facing poverty. Black people and other people of color more often live in communities that are physically cut off from the economic and power centers of society, through urban planning and political decisions past and present. This arresting of social mobility is no accident.[24]

Black people are also limited in public spaces because of safety. With each news report of a Black person killed by law enforcement or harmed by White community members, the emotional and psychological scars lead to fear about our own public safety.

Black people and other people of color face unsolicited and profound obstacles reflecting structural racism and White supremacy in policy, planning, design, engineering, and law enforcement.

Black people are less likely to have unimpeded access to critical resources and everyday destinations such as grocery stores, healthcare facilities, schools, parks and open spaces, and jobs.

The lack of mobility affects physical health. The National Health Interview Survey found that between 2006 and 2015, Black, Asian, and Hispanic people "were significantly less likely to engage in sufficient physical activity compared with [non-Hispanic] Whites."[25] The Centers for Disease Control reports that Black adults are 1.2 times more likely to die of heart disease than White adults.[26] The public health field links these statistics to the social determinants of health, which are the factors in one's environment—where they live, work, play, and age—and how those affect one's health.[27]

This book won't be going deeply into the social determinants of health, but they are important indicators of what happens when we design our cities and communities and enact laws and social norms that create enormous barriers to mobility for Black Americans.

THE FOUR Ps: POLITY, POLICY, PLANNING, AND POLICING

Society has created barriers to mobility for Black people through what I call "The Four Ps": polity, policy, planning, and policing. All of these "Ps" are a manner of policing Black people's behaviors, just through different means—some less overtly violent but all harmful in distinct ways.

It all begins with ***polity***, which consists of the social forces and governance structures that create a separate set of rules for Black and non-Black people. Our polity has been shaped over centuries of written and unwritten rules that guide how people engage within our society. Our polity shapes how the government enacts laws, how laws are maintained and enforced, and the unwritten social codes linked to societal behavior. At a basic level, polity is a nation, a city, a church—a collective identity.

Beyond the laws, the collective actions of dominant groups have maintained the polity. White neighbors have long played a role in arresting the mobility of Black people through threats and harassment. This enforcement by the community creates a hostile environment that reinforces racial boundaries and restricts the freedoms of Black people.

Policy refers to legislation and laws that create conditions of arrested mobility. These are the rules and regulations shaped by the structures that a polity establishes. For instance, policies such as redlining have historically been used to confine Black people to certain neighborhoods and prevent them from moving freely within a city. These policies were designed not just to segregate but to control and limit the economic, social, and physical mobility of Black communities. Even when explicit laws were removed, the legacy of these policies continues to arrest the mobility of Black people, as the very structures and practices they created still influence who has access to resources and opportunities.

The organization of our communities is determined by urban ***planning***, which is practiced at the federal, state, local (county, city, or other municipality), and regional government levels. Decisions about zoning, land use, urban design, transportation, and engineering all shape the physical and social structure of communities. They can have a profound impact on issues such as mobility, access to resources, and overall quality of life for Black Americans.

And finally, ***policing*** is how law enforcement is used to enforce policy and planning practices. The way policing is enacted depends on the polity, the overall culture and expectations of a populace. Sarah A. Seo, author of *Policing the Open Road: How Cars Transformed American Freedom*, shows how the history of driving and policing are deeply connected. In the early twentieth century, traffic norms were enforced through citizen groups, but with the mass production of the automobile there was an "immediate imperative to regulate the motoring public," Seo explains. "The law's accommodation of discretionary policing profoundly altered what it meant to live free from state intrusion in the Automobile Age."[28,29]

"Before cars, American police had more in common with their eighteenth-century forebears than with their twentieth-century successors. What revolutionized policing was a technological innovation that would come to define the new century."[30] There were traffic regulations in place at the advent of the automobile, but almost nobody followed them, which resulted in a lot of property damage, injury, and death. "It soon became clear that the public's interest in street and highway safety required more policing," writes Seo. "The police power not only authorized social and economic regulations; it also sanctioned the police's power. In other words, the breathtaking expansion of the police rested on the same public rights that gave rise to the modern administrative state."[31]

Citizens still police the movements and activities of other citizens. This is most often seen in how White citizens police the behavior, and sometimes existence, of Black citizens in public.

The concept of arrested mobility can help planners, policymakers, and the general public understand the social and political forces that lead to a lack of mobility—both physical and social—for Black people and other people of color. By understanding the causes, we have more tools to create solutions that directly address mobility for Black people, other people of color, and other marginalized groups.

It's important to note that we cannot and should not cast Black Americans as helpless people who must be "saved." Throughout the book, I've focused on the leadership and resilience of the Black community that is leading efforts for solutions to un-arrest mobility.

For me, arrested mobility is a chronic disease—a condition with deep-rooted causes and acute impacts, disproportionately targeting Black people. To treat this disease, we must first diagnose it accurately, something most discussions fail to do. In the first half of this book, I diagnose the problem, exposing the mechanisms that have systematically limited Black mobility. This will give you an unflinching look at what needs to be dismantled.

But diagnosis alone isn't enough; we must also pursue solutions, which I explore in the last two chapters.

The cure requires more than just acknowledgment; it demands action. We must penalize discriminatory enforcement, invest in Black communities, enact equitable policies, empower community voices, expand educational and economic opportunities, raise public awareness, and provide essential mental and physical health resources. Only then can we begin to reverse the damage of arrested mobility and create lasting change by *un*-arresting the mobility for all Black Americans.

Change is possible, and it starts with all of us.

ONE

How Arrested Mobility Is Created Through Polity and Policy

"Racism is not merely a simplistic hatred. It is, more often, broad sympathy toward some and broader skepticism toward others. Black America ever lives under that skeptical eye."
—Ta-Nehisi Coates, *Between the World and Me*

Arrested mobility of Black Americans is tightly wound into our country's institutions through systemic racism. When it is not overt, the effects of arrested mobility often remain invisible to people who don't directly experience them. To change the system and reshape our communities so they are safe and livable for people of all races, we must understand what shaped them in the first place and how it arrested the mobility of Black Americans.

Some of the rules we live by have been formalized through governance structures such as the US Constitution, but some are less tangible and are more ingrained in what society deems as appropriate, civilized behavior.

Because race is such an important undercurrent to how our country came to be, it has shaped almost everything in how the public engages with

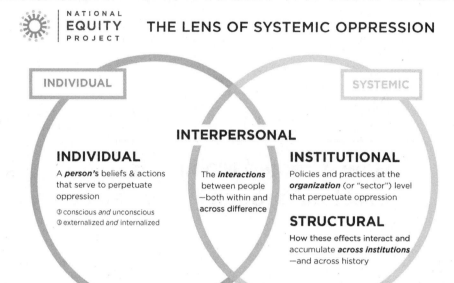

FIGURE 1-1 This diagram from the National Equity Project shows how the four forms of racism interact with one another. (Image courtesy of National Equity Project 2018, https://www.nationalequityproject.org/frameworks/lens-of-systemic-oppression)

social codes. To understand our polity—the social forces that shape how we are governed and what set of rules we follow—we must first understand the four types of racism: *individual, interpersonal, institutional,* and *structural* (Figure 1-1).

INDIVIDUAL RACISM

Individual racism describes a person's beliefs and actions about other people, particularly people of a group different from their own. Often people are not conscious of those beliefs when they're infused through the default culture. For example, thinking of what is considered "professional" office culture, the standard almost everywhere in the United States is based on White cultural norms. This dictates what is expected in how a worker dresses, how they speak, and certain formalities. If a person of color does not match these expectations, such as a Black woman coming to work with locs or a braided hairstyle rather than straightened hair, a colleague or boss might see this as a lack of professionalism. That assessment might feel neutral because it's couched in standards of professionalism, but when the norms are rooted in White standards, it is a form of individual racism.

When people of color absorb individual racist viewpoints because of the White-dominant cultural norms all around them, it is known as internalized racism. "In a society where racial prejudice thrives in politics, communities, institutions and popular culture, it's difficult for people of color to avoid absorbing the racist messages that constantly bombard them," wrote Nadra Kareem Nittle in *ThoughtCo*.[1] For example, a Black woman may feel pressure to hold up the White standards of "professionalism" by changing her hairstyle for the workplace.

When the dominant culture is rooted in Whiteness, that becomes the standard by which all judgments are made, resulting in *individual and internalized racism*. In a world where concepts of "colorblindness" such as messages of "I don't see race" are pervasive, they are not recognizing or acknowledging the racism behind these standards.

INTERPERSONAL RACISM

Internalized racism never stays internal; rather, it guides actions and interactions, or *interpersonal racism*.

Examples of interpersonal racism can be extreme, such as the lynching of Black Americans in the nineteenth and twentieth centuries and modern-day hate crimes.

Interpersonal racism can also be subtle, such as through microaggressions, which are everyday interactions based on a bias or stereotype that largely go unnoticed by the aggressor. Examples include a person moving to the other side of the street when they see a Black person walking toward them, comments on a Black person being "surprisingly articulate," or critiquing a Black woman for being "too aggressive" in her interaction. In the workplace example of individual racism, interpersonal racism could be underhanded comments about the lack of professionalism in wearing her hair in braids or locs.

The subtler forms of interpersonal racism can lead to harmful and often dangerous circumstances for many Black people. In schools, Black students' behavior is often judged much more harshly than that of their White peers, leading to more severe and higher rates of punishment. In a 2021 study published in *American Psychologist*, researchers found that among 2,381 students (35% Black, 65% White) from twelve schools in a district, the Black students reported much higher suspension rates for minor infractions. Twenty-six percent of the Black students reported suspensions, and only 2 percent of White students did.[2]

"Unfortunately, we were not surprised by the findings, considering what we know about the role of racial bias in painting school adults' views of African American youth as less innocent, older and more aggressive than their white peers," says study co-author and professor of psychology at the University of Pittsburgh Ming-Te Wang. "Regardless of the behavior that African American youth engage in, that behavior is viewed by educators as more worthy of harsh school discipline like a suspension."[3]

Interpersonal discrimination also shows up in healthcare. According to a 2018 *California Health Report* article, Black mothers are "least likely to be listened to," which in turn affects the health of the patients and can increase the risk of death during pregnancy.[4] This fact gained national attention when Serena Williams almost died after her daughter was born.[5]

Similarly, Black Americans are undertreated for pain. Sophie Trawalter, professor and social psychologist at the University of Virginia, conducted various studies about biases in patient care, finding in a study of medical students that "for those who have these beliefs that biological differences are real, we see the predicted bias where these participants saying or reporting that White patients would feel more pain than Black patients."[6] Yet Trawalter notes that some studies have found that Black patients in reality report more pain than White patients, which highlights provider biases. This finding shows how internalized racism leads to interpersonal racism that endangers patients when enacted in healthcare settings.

We also know through the seemingly endless list of names of Black Americans taken from this Earth too soon, whether at the hands of police or self-deputized White citizens, because internalized racism led to interpersonal racism.

INSTITUTIONAL RACISM

Institutional racism is racism that is normalized through policies, practices, and discriminatory treatment that creates barriers to opportunity within an organization or institution.

Institutional racism is seen in racial profiling by the police, unequal access to educational and employment opportunities, discriminatory treatment by healthcare professionals, and discrimination in the education system, to name a few examples. What makes these institutional instead of interpersonal is that they are rooted in the practices and policies that are accepted by the institutions.

In the example of professional expectations about women's hairstyles, it becomes institutional racism when workplace rules prohibit braids or locs. For example, until 2017 the US Army enforced a no-loc or dreadlock policy in its grooming standards for hairstyles while in uniform.[7] Although the policy was deemed neutral because it applied to everyone serving in the Army, it predominantly affected Black people.

In educational institutions, punishing Black students more harshly than White students (interpersonal racism) becomes institutional racism when the policies allow for harsher punishment of Black students. A zero-tolerance policy, which punishes students for minor infractions such as dress code violations, texting, or talking out of turn in class, is an example of an institutional policy that reinforces racial stereotypes when enforced inequitably.

"On the surface, zero tolerance policies are facially neutral; they are to apply equally to all regardless of race, class and gender," writes Nancy Heitzeg, professor of sociology and program director of critical studies of race and ethnicity at St. Catherine University in the journal *Contemporary Justice Review*. "A growing body of research suggests that these policies are anything but."[8] Ming-Te Wang's study shows that Black students are much more likely to be harshly punished for these zero-tolerance policies than White students. The researchers found that harsh punishment based on racial bias takes a toll on Black students, leading to lower grades and a rupture in the students' trust and relationship with educators and the education system as a whole.[9] Heitzeg also found that "zero tolerance policies contribute to the already high drop-out rate for students of color."[10]

In healthcare there is a fine line between interpersonal and institutional racism. Healthcare systems don't institutionalize policies that dictate less pain management for Black patients, for example. But the racism becomes institutional when little is done to combat how unconscious bias and interpersonal racism affect the quality of healthcare that Black people receive. The gaps in care often become justified because the provider has medical expertise.

In law enforcement, policies, laws, and practices are used to justify racial profiling, and the lack of accountability for law enforcement makes it difficult to get justice for Black people shot by police. In the employment sector, there is a perception of objectivity through steps applicants must take in the hiring process, but bias is still present. A 2021 study by the National Bureau of Economic Research found that applicants with "distinctively Black names" were 10 percent less likely to receive callbacks.[11]

STRUCTURAL RACISM

Racism becomes *structural* when institutional racism accumulates over time and across institutions. This happens when White cultural norms are accepted as "the" cultural norms and are embedded in societal practices.

The accumulated effect of institutional racism toward Black students in schools affects their social and economic mobility because they are held back at every step. When Black patients face discrimination in healthcare and thus receive lower-quality care, it affects their overall well-being.

The media also has a hand in perpetuating systemic racism. "Media generated hysteria inextricably linked 'teen super-predators,' gang-violence and the crack cocaine 'epidemic,' and all were unmistakably characterized as issues of race," wrote Heitzeg. "The coverage of the youth gangs, which focused almost exclusively on African American and Latino gangs, exaggerated the extent of gang membership and gang violence, contributing the creation of 'moral panic.'"[12] That moral panic then leads to systemic racism that makes Black people less safe in public because White-dominant norms have embedded the idea that they are dangerous. Structural racism affects the physical and social mobility of Black people.

In Noxubee County, where my hometown of Shuqualak, Mississippi, is, public schools are predominantly Black, which has led to disinvestment. Noxubee County School District has been significantly underfunded: Over $13 million should have gone to Noxubee County students since 2008.[13]

This is an example of systemic racism because it's accepted by decision-makers in Noxubee County that predominantly Black schools will be underfunded, and there will be no consequences. In 2024, a decision by the Mississippi State Supreme Court allowed pandemic relief funds to go to the Midsouth Association of Independent Schools (which oversees 125 private schools in Mississippi), channeling more public funds to private education.[14] Public school funding is contested all over the country, but the racial implications in Mississippi are stark. As of 2016, 87 percent of private school enrollment in Mississippi consisted of White students when only 51 percent of school-aged kids were White.[15] This is the largest disparity between Black and White students enrolled in private schools in the United States, where the national average is 15 percent. Public schools in Mississippi have been underfunded for decades, yet the state is spending more of its meager education funds on mostly White private schools. This is a prime example of structural racism.

Laws and policies that overlook predominantly Black communities have long-lasting consequences. Poor road conditions, lack of sidewalks, and limited access to safe and efficient public transportation arrest the mobility of Black residents and contribute to the physical and social isolation.

SEPARATE BUT PARALLEL SYSTEMS

Racism in all its forms has created a situation where Black mobility is affected at every step. Despite living in the same society, Black people live in a different system than White people.

The separate but parallel roads are apt metaphors when we're talking about mobility. The two roads are built and maintained differently from one another, and that affects the people who walk, drive, or move along those roads (as illustrated in Figure 1-2). Certainly, it is an oversimplification because experiences vary from individual to individual, but it is a helpful way to look at the different roads Black and White Americans travel.

Legislative actions have attempted to correct harms done, including through the Civil Rights Act of 1964, the Voting Rights Act of 1965, the Fair Housing Act of 1968, the Equal Opportunity Employer Act of 1970, the Americans with Disabilities Act of 1990, the National Voter Registration Act of 1993, and the Transportation Equity Act for the 21st Century of 1998. In 2023, the Biden administration signed two executive orders committing to environmental justice. Through the Justice40 Initiative, the administration will commit 40 percent of infrastructure and climate resilience spending to disadvantaged and marginalized communities.[16] These actions by the president and Congress recognize that action at the federal level

FIGURE 1-2 White Roads and Black roads are not built the same. (a) The White road is fairly straight. (b) The Black road is much longer and more circuitous than the White road. This road metaphor is ironic because enslaved Black Americans literally built the foundations of the infrastructure we use today in the United States—the roads, the railroads, the buildings. (Illustration by Tom Grillo)

was needed to improve the road for Black Americans—ironic because the federal government played a role in creating these disparities and inequities. Many of these acts of Congress came out of the activism of Black Americans and calls for justice. It's unlikely any of these would have taken place without our agency. Yet challenges remain because they cannot address the roots of systemic racism that is so strong in our institutions.

Policing

Black people are policed more heavily than White Americans.

One in two young Black men will experience arrest by age 23. In 2016, 27 percent of arrests were of Black people despite Black people making up only 13 percent of the US population. Black people were arrested 2.12 times more often than White people for "drug abuse."[17]

Black people are much more likely to experience traffic stops, and Black and Hispanic drivers are more often subject to searches than White drivers.[18] (I get into this topic in greater detail later in the book.)

Reed T. DeAngelis, a population health scientist at the University of Michigan and formerly a postdoctoral researcher at Duke University, where he conducted research using the Mapping Police Violence dataset, says, "The threshold for being perceived as dangerous, and thereby falling victim to lethal police force, appears to be higher for White civilians relative to their Black or Hispanic peers."[19]

The overpolicing of Black Americans has led to an incarceration rate for Black Americans that is five times higher than that of White Americans. One in 81 Black adults have served time in state prison.[20]

Nazgol Ghandnoosh and Celeste Berry of the Sentencing Project write, "Police officers' reliance on millions of minor traffic stops annually as a pretext to investigate drivers for criminal activity disproportionately impacts Black and Latinx drivers."[21]

The challenge is complex and requires a multilayered response. Ghandnoosh and Berry write, "Ending racial inequity in the criminal legal system requires both effectively tackling disparities in serious criminal behavior and eliminating excessive police contact."

There are unwritten rules by which Black citizens must live that White citizens don't have to think about (represented in Figure 1-2 by the speed limit signs, with Black drivers being held to a lower speed limit). There is an old adage that Black parents tell their kids to "be twice as good" in order to succeed. "Twice as smart, twice as dependable, twice as talented," wrote Gillian B. White in *The Atlantic*.[22] Black parents don't need the data to tell them that the rules don't apply the same way to their kids. They know because they experienced it.

Access to Capital

In my community, confidence in obtaining access to capital from banks or credit unions—even when fully qualified—was so limited when I was growing up that I never imagined it was possible. The denials were constant, even for homeowners. To us, banks were nothing more than a place to deposit money, not a means to build wealth or secure a better future.

There is a long history of financial exclusion and systemic racism in access to capital. The legacy of the Freedman's Savings Bank, which failed Black Americans after the Civil War, loomed large. It left a lasting distrust in financial institutions, a distrust that was reinforced every time someone was denied a loan or capital, regardless of their qualifications. As a result, many in my community turned to hiding their savings under mattresses—literally and figuratively locking away their potential—because they believed the doors to financial opportunity were firmly shut to them. This reality not only arrests our economic mobility but also stunts our belief in the possibility of anything different.

In a 2021 Brookings study, "Long Shadows," researchers Scott Winship, Christopher Pulliam, Ariel Gelrud Shiro, Richard V. Reeves, and Santiago Deambrosi determined that Black adults over thirty years old were over sixteen times more likely to experience third-generation poverty than White adults. "In other words," Winship et al. noted, "experiencing poverty for three generations straight is almost uniquely a Black experience."[23]

Most Black Americans start the road with less money at their disposal because previous generations were robbed of wealth that could have been passed on to future generations (represented by the beginning of the road where it's broken and cracked in Figure 1-2b). Their homes and communities were devalued by redlining in the early twentieth century, so they couldn't secure fair and affordable mortgages, and later their homes were destroyed during the urban renewal era to build freeways and expand development.[24,25]

During this period of history, there were structures in place to help struggling Americans, specifically after the Great Depression, but Black Americans received less aid or were completely excluded from programs, including those to aid in homeownership.[26] So the means by which White Americans were able to build wealth were the same means that cut off access to wealth for Black Americans (the high cost of housing and education for Black Americans is represented by the tollbooth causing a backup of cars in Figure 1-2b).[27]

Because of these historical wrongs, Black Americans are still less likely to own homes than White Americans. Rashawn Ray, Andre M. Perry, David Harshbarger, and Samantha Elizondo of the Brookings Institution note that as of 2021, only 46.4 percent of Black Americans own homes, whereas 75 percent of White families do.[28]

"Compounding matters, homes in predominately Black neighborhoods across the country are valued at $48,000 less than predominately white neighborhoods for a cumulative loss in equity of approximately $156 billion," they write.

When a Black person on our metaphorical road reaches the tollbooth representing higher education, their lack of accumulated generational wealth requires them to borrow much more money. In effect, the cost of higher education is much higher for them than for their White peers. Of course, the cost of higher education and ballooning student loan debt is growing across the board, but it affects Black Americans most. According to the US Department of Education, Black graduates take out on average $25,000 more in student loan debt than their White counterparts, and after four years Black students owe an average of 188 percent more than White students.[29] Thus, Black Americans accumulate more interest and pay more over time.

Because of the lack of generational wealth and structural racism entrenched in the lending system, Black Americans are less likely to have high credit scores and thus less able to attain fair and affordable mortgages.[30] "Lower average credit scores not only make it more difficult for Black people to achieve homeownership," write Michelle Aronowitz, Edward L. Golding, and Jung Hyun Choi in a report from the MIT Golub Center for Finance and Policy, "but also contribute to homeownership being more costly for Black people after it's been attained."[31] This is but one of many financial burdens placed on Black Americans when it comes to home ownership. The authors go on to note that Black Americans pay higher rates to mortgage companies because of "perceived risk factors," Black borrowers don't have equal access to refinancing opportunities, Black borrowers pay higher mortgage insurance rates, and Black homeowners bear a higher property tax burden.

So not only do Black homeowners have less access to generational wealth to buy a house, but when they actually do get that opportunity, they end up paying much more than White homeowners.

Toxic Stress

Growing up in Shuqualak, I vividly remember when the glove factory and the Piggly Wiggly grocery store shut their doors for good. These weren't just businesses; they were lifelines in our small town, anchoring the local economy and providing a sense of financial stability. Their closures sent shockwaves through our community, triggering economic paralysis and unleashing a surge of toxic stress. The toxic stress that permeates daily life is not just an emotional burden; it's a destructive force that erodes the fabric of a community, leaving a legacy of trauma that stifles progress and perpetuates a cycle of poverty and hopelessness.

The loss of these economic anchors was devastating, underscoring the urgent need for renewal and investment to break free from this vicious cycle. Arrested mobility and toxic stress are a deadly combination.

Leila Morsy and Richard Rothstein of the Economic Policy Institute found that children growing up in lower-income settings from infancy are "more likely to have strong, frequent, or prolonged exposure to major traumatic events."[32] This can induce a stress response, often called "toxic stress," leading to negative outcomes including depression, behavior challenges, lower academic performance, and poor health (represented in Figure 1-2b by the long, uneven, unpaved stretch of road). The study notes that Black children are "45 percent more likely than white children to be exposed to one frightening and threatening experience."

Valentina Lagomarsino from Harvard University writes that biological changes occur in the brains of children who experience toxic stress. "Adverse childhood events, including racism, community violence, loss of a parent due to police brutality, poverty, and even the mental state of a child's parent have been shown to cause toxic stress."[33]

Race-Neutral Policies

Race-neutral policies, also known as colorblind policies, are those that don't address race or racism in their design (represented by construction in Figure 1-2). Examples of race-neutral policies include many of the acts of Congress designed to right the wrongs of the past, such as those listed at the beginning of the section on separate but parallel systems. When they take a race-neutral approach, they're not going to go far enough.

"The Fair Housing Act only mitigated the harm inflicted on communities of color by outlawing future racist policies," wrote Adewale A. Maye of the Economic Policy Institute. "The act did not tackle the residential patterns—such as the segregation into neighborhoods with lower price appreciation and less investment—that resulted from the past policies."[34]

There are examples in education as well. In June 2023, the Supreme Court effectively reversed affirmative action, a policy that acknowledged the history of race and racism in college admissions. With this reversal, we're potentially moving to an era of race-neutral college admissions.[35] As I write this, it's uncertain how colleges and universities will respond, but knowing what we do about achievement disparities caused by historical racism, there is no such thing as an even playing field when it comes to race.

"These race-neutral policies neglect the reality and history of race and the role it has played in stripping communities of color from opportunity," writes Maye. "Our country isn't race-neutral despite efforts to push race-neutral policy. Without targeted policies to address the structural barriers in access and equity, lawmakers will struggle to advance restorative policies that can truly combat racial disparities."[36]

Although there is movement toward acknowledging and addressing racial disparities, there is a long way to go.

Community as Solidarity and Resilience

Community as part of the Black experience is an essential component to moving forward along any road.

"'It takes a village' is a proverb that has been attributed to African cultures," wrote Triesta Fowler, scientific diversity officer for the National Institute on Minority Health and Health Disparities (NIMHD), and Monica Webb Hooper, deputy director of NIMHD, in the National Institutes of

Health *Musings from the Mezzanine*.[37] "This belief in the power of community is an important component and strength of African American culture. . . . Members of the village become part of a redefined extended family that share a common culture, values, and customs. These members may include other relatives, close friends, neighbors, and a trusted religious community. These connections have been defined as 'fictive kin,'[38] or people who reinforce and extend the familial bonds beyond a biological relationship."

There is no better example of this familial bond than through mutual aid that has been a part of the Black American experience since the times of enslavement. Mutual aid is solidarity-based support networks built by collective community action to support neighbors and the community writ large. It is driven by people donating goods, funds, or time to help others. During the COVID pandemic, mutual aid became essential for people who had lost their jobs or who were immunocompromised and could not leave the house to meet their basic needs. The concept was coined by anarchist philosopher Peter Kropotkin, who recognized our inherent inclination to care for one another in his book *Mutual Aid: A Factor of Evolution*.[39] The idea of mutual aid has strong roots in Black communities, which built community resilience when society failed to support them. It subverts the charity model that typically requires the "haves" giving to the "have-nots." It is built on horizontal means of solidarity, recognizing the power in collective action, support, and connection.

Ariel Aberg-Riger detailed some historic examples of mutual aid networks in *Bloomberg CityLab*, including the Free African Society, one of many Black mutual aid societies that was essential in caring for the sick, housing orphaned children, and burying the dead during the 1793 yellow fever outbreak.[40] In 1969 in Philadelphia the Black Panthers started a free breakfast program. There are many smaller, localized networks in Black communities to help with childcare, food, housing, and other basic needs of survival.

In addition to mutual aid networks, there are the countless Black community members—teachers, librarians, business owners, nonprofit leaders—who use their success and their position to empower and support younger generations. This support is symbolized on the metaphorical road by a tow truck, or by someone stopping to help after a fender bender, rebuilding a road, or removing the debris to allow others to pass.

These actions show the power of community in surviving and thriving on a harrowing and difficult journey. The street festival in Figure 1-2b represents the power of resilience and self-determination.

It was the innumerable Black community members—principals, teachers, business owners, elected officials, and grandmothers—who became the lifeline that saved me, my siblings, and many others in our community from the grip of arrested mobility. Their success was not just personal; they used their positions to empower and uplift the younger generations, providing us with the mentorship, support, and resources that so many others lacked.

On my block alone in Shuqualak, MS, these role models and community pillars nurtured and inspired a generation that went on to become doctors, professors, business owners, firefighters, high-level government employees, teachers, lawyers, barbers, truckers, coaches, and more. We are the exception, not the rule, in a system designed to hold us back. But it was through their relentless commitment to our futures, their belief in our potential, and their willingness to invest in us that we were able to break free from the constraints that ensnare so many others.

Black Americans have built up a great amount of resilience over the centuries of oppression. Even though the roads and the conditions were different and more treacherous for Black people, they were able to thrive by supporting one another. And in some cases, Black Americans built vibrant, economically prosperous communities after enslavement, such as in Wilmington, North Carolina, and Tulsa, Oklahoma's Greenwood District. But in both cases, resentment and hatred by White residents led to the only successful coup in American history in Wilmington (a buried piece of history covered in *Scene on Radio*'s "Echoes of a Coup" series[41]) and to the massacre of about 300 people, with 800 injured, in the 1921 Tulsa Race Massacre.[42] Even amid the violence and intimidation, Black Americans have consistently fought for our rights while also building strong, cohesive, and resilient communities.

In order to truly repair the harms caused over centuries, we *all* need to focus on un-arresting the mobility of Black people.

By un-arresting mobility, we have an opportunity to create a better society not just for Black people but for all people. Arrested mobility is bad for our society as a whole, not just the people it directly harms. By not providing equitable access to jobs, community resources, and public spaces, we are limiting the potential of a large percentage of our population to participate and contribute to society. In *The Sum of Us*, Heather McGhee argues that the zero-sum mentality perpetuated by racism has led to disinvestment in resources for all people, not just people of color, noting that we all lose by either intentionally or unintentionally maintaining systemic racism.[43] "A functioning society rests on a web of mutuality, a willingness among all involved to share enough with one another to accomplish what no one person can do alone," she writes. "In a sense, that's what government is."[44] But when policies are created through a lens of racism, White people lose out as well.

In fact, the major bank Citigroup put a concrete number on this loss to society in a 2020 study. As a result of discrimination against Black Americans, the US gross domestic product lost some $16 trillion between 2000 and 2020.[45]

This puts a fine point on how our economy suffers and, along with it, our community vitality and our connection to one another when the mobility of Black people and other people of color is arrested. By correcting issues of social and physical mobility for Black Americans, we can create a more vibrant, diverse, connected, and successful society for everyone.

TWO

The Urban Planning Strategies That Have Shaped Our Communities

"Urban renewal . . . means negro removal."
—James Baldwin, 1963

In 2016, thirty-two-year-old Philando Castile, who was Black, was pulled over by a police officer in Falcon Heights, Minnesota, a suburb of St. Paul. After he informed the officer that he had a firearm and that he wasn't pulling it out, the officer shot and killed Castile as he reached for his identification. His girlfriend was in the passenger seat of the car.

In 2020, twenty-five-year-old Ahmaud Arbery, who was Black, went for a run in the Satilla Shores neighborhood in Glynn County, Georgia. Suspected of being a burglar, he was chased by three White men, tackled, and then shot and killed by one of the men.

In 2023, sixteen-year-old Ralph Yarl, who is Black, drove to pick up his brother from a friend's house in Kansas City, Missouri. After ringing the bell of the wrong house, he was shot by the homeowner, an eighty-four-year-old White man. Unlike Arbery, Yarl survived with two gunshot wounds to the head.

These names have become well known among Americans. They are just a few of the hundreds of Black people moving about America who have been shot by the police or by self-deputized community members who suspect anyone who does not look like them.

The White-centric planning and design of our cities and communities have led to racial segregation and created circumstances for Black and Brown people to be targeted as they move through White-dominated spaces. Although much of the segregation of communities is a result of early- to mid-twentieth-century planning, these practices are perpetuated when planning is not carried out through a lens of race and racial equity. Scholar Richard Rothstein wrote of residential segregation in *The Color of Law: A Forgotten History of How Our Government Segregated America*, "The policy was so systematic and forceful that its effects endure to the present time. Without our government's purposeful imposition of racial segregation, the other causes—private prejudice, white flight, real estate steering, bank redlining, income differences and self-segregation—still would have existed but with far less opportunity for expression."[1]

Many planning or policy decisions were thinly veiled acts of racism by government-run organizations to segregate communities by race and class. Some actions were more overt, what Rothstein and others call de jure segregation, which is "segregation by intentional government action."[2] Even when segregation was no longer written into law, the circumstances created by planning and policy decisions reinforced segregation and made way for the disinvestment and destruction of Black and Brown communities.

When planners and policymakers fail to look at land use regulations, laws enacted through public policy, and urban design through the lens of un-arresting mobility for Black citizens, they continue to perpetuate segregation, discrimination, and the overpolicing of Black bodies.

We need to understand the decisions that got us here.

THE HISTORY OF ARRESTED MOBILITY THROUGH LAND USE REGULATIONS

While I was growing up in Shuqualak, Mississippi, my family warned me to avoid the "other side of the tracks," particularly at night. Across the tracks was a predominantly White community where a Black kid like me could expect to be treated with suspicion and judgment.

It was only when I grew up, traveled outside Mississippi, and became a planner that I started to understand neighborhoods like mine were considered to be the *other* side of the tracks. I began to see the disrepair, the lack of maintenance, and the disregard of Black communities. I saw the way that mobility is arrested for Black people on both sides of the tracks. On my side, upward mobility was arrested.

Take, for example, the location of any corridor named after Dr. Martin Luther King, Jr. in US cities. A 2020 study found that "poverty rates are almost double the national average in areas surrounding streets named after Martin Luther King Jr.," and educational attainment is much lower. The communities surrounding these streets are predominantly African American.[3] These communities lack investment and therefore are often deemed "unsafe." One very visual piece of evidence is the lack of trees or tree cover in those other-side-of-the-track neighborhoods. In fact, studies have shown that wealthy (and thanks to generational wealth, majority White) neighborhoods have 50 percent more greenery than lower-income neighborhoods.[4]

Understanding the harms perpetuated through segregation by way of zoning and land use regulations, displacement of Black and Brown communities through urban renewal projects, and other ways that we implement policy and plan our cities is essential to un-arresting Black mobility.

Zoning, Regulations, and Segregation

Zoning has been a powerful tool of segregation.

The legal definition of zoning makes it sound straightforward: "a legislative act dividing a jurisdiction's land into sections and regulating different land uses in each section in accordance with a zoning ordinance."[5]

"It's kind of the DNA of our built environment," says Jocelyn Gibson from Cincinnati ZoneCo, a firm of interdisciplinary code writers focused on equitable and resilient zoning.[6,7] "Your DNA is something that's working behind the scenes. What you look like, your personality, so many things about yourself are determined by your DNA. In communities it's this thing that's underlying a set of rules that's sort of deciding how the built environment manifests. How tall can your building be? What is the setback from the street? What is the minimum lot size? The uses that are permitted on that property. Could you put a factory on it? Could you put a restaurant on it? Could you put a home on it, an apartment building? What can you do with that property? What's permitted?"

M. Nolan Gray, who is a former graduate intern of mine at Rutgers University, writes in his book *Arbitrary Lines: How Zoning Broke the American City and How to Fix It*, "Until recently, zoning might have been blithely dismissed as a mere technical matter, simply a way of rationalizing our cities, a planning policy so obvious as to be beyond reproach. But zoning is at once so much less and so much more. While occasionally used as a stand-in for city planning or building regulations more broadly, its scope is far more limited: at a basic level, all zoning does is segregate land uses and regulate densities."[8]

Zoning, Gray notes, is anything but benign. "In most major cities, zoning restricts roughly three-quarters of the city to low-slung single-family housing, banning apartments altogether," he writes. The prevalence of communities with low-density housing that is exclusively single family has raised the median housing prices dramatically and contributed to the incredible wealth gap.[9]

Rothstein describes the "problems" that concerned these segregationists: "how to keep lower-income African Americans from living near middle-class whites and how to keep middle-class African Americans from buying into white middle-class neighborhoods."[10] Rothstein explains that cities such as St. Louis used zoning ordinances and deed restrictions as a way to skirt the law. The architect behind these thinly veiled racist maneuvers was the city's planning engineer, Harland Bartholomew. He strategically controlled who could purchase homes by zoning White neighborhoods for single-family homes or "residential-first," thereby making them unaffordable to lower-income families. This effectively created segregation.

Heather Worthington of Worthington Advisors, a community engagement and consulting firm in Minneapolis, explains how deed restrictions were used by White community members to keep Black families from moving into their neighborhoods. "In most of the most desirable neighborhoods in Minneapolis—especially around lakes, we have these really beautiful urban lakes—all the neighborhoods that were built in the nineteen-teens and twenties were deed-restricted. We started looking at that data and realized that the zoning information that we had going back to the mid-1920s closely paralleled those deed restrictions," she says.[11] "What was happening was that developers were using the deed restrictions and the city was coming in behind them and zoning them single-family. And the result was that those neighborhoods were completely closed to people of color."[12]

In the mid-1920s, many cities were adopting racial zoning laws that barred Black residents from purchasing homes in White neighborhoods.[13] Although the 1917 Supreme Court decision *Buchanan v. Warley* states that a ban on the sale of real estate to Black people violates freedom of contract, as protected under the Fourteenth Amendment, many states ignored the ruling.[14] Richard D. Kahlenberg, senior fellow at the Century Foundation says, "The Buchanan decision had the immediate effect of striking down numerous racial zoning ordinances, including those in cities from Atlanta and Baltimore to New Orleans and St. Louis. However, communities quickly circumvented the ruling by adopting economic zoning laws that effectively excluded the vast majority of African Americans (along with economically disadvantaged whites)."[15]

Homeownership was expensive for working-class and middle-class people, including White families. To help more Americans achieve home ownership, the Franklin D. Roosevelt administration created the Home Owners' Loan Corporation (HOLC) in 1933, which refinanced home mortgages that were in default and expanded home-buying opportunities. These benefits were not extended to Black Americans. "The HOLC created color-coded maps of every metropolitan area in the nation, with the safest neighborhoods colored green and the riskiest colored red," wrote Rothstein. "A neighborhood earned a red color if African Americans lived in it, even if it was a solid middle-class neighborhood of single-family homes."[16] This is where the term *redlining* came from.

To buy a home, Black Americans had to enter into risky real estate agreements such as buying "on contract." Ta-Nehisi Coates describes this particular form of predatory practice in his seminal story for *The Atlantic*, "The Case for Reparations," through the journey to home ownership of Clyde Ross in the North Lawndale neighborhood of Chicago in 1961.[17]

The seller bought the home for $12,000 and sold it to Ross six months later for $27,500. "In a contract sale, the seller kept the deed until the contract was paid in full—and, unlike with a normal mortgage, Ross would acquire no equity in the meantime," wrote Coates. "If he missed a single payment, he would immediately forfeit his $1,000 down payment, all his monthly payments, and the property itself. The men who peddled contracts in North Lawndale would sell homes at inflated prices and then evict fami-

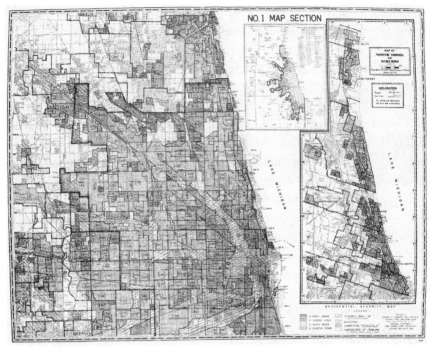

FIGURE 2-1 HOLC map of Chicago. "A First Grade" is classified as "best" according to HOLC, "B Second Grade" is "still desirable," "C Third Grade" is "definitely declining," and "D Fourth Grade" is "hazardous." (Source: Mapping Inequality, public domain image)

lies who could not pay—taking their down payment and their monthly installments as profit. Then they'd bring in another black family, rinse, and repeat."

Redlining, tacitly condoned by the US government, stripped Black Americans from building generational wealth through home ownership. And because redlined neighborhoods were deemed "risky," those communities experienced disinvestment by local and community governments (Figure 2-1). "Redlining destroyed the possibility of investment wherever black people lived," wrote Coates.

"The combination of deed restrictions, zoning, and redlining were a very effective block to people of color purchasing property and moving into those neighborhoods," Worthington told me.

Some Black redlined neighborhoods showed incredible resilience in the face of a system created to keep them down. Many redlined neighborhoods became thriving centers of Black resilience, as evidenced by the evolution of the jazz scene in the twentieth century. The three cities *DownBeat Magazine* recognized as center stage for developing jazz in the United States are New Orleans, New York, and Chicago.[18] In New York it was Harlem[19]; in New Orleans it was multiple neighborhoods including Tremé, Central City, and the sixth through ninth wards[20]; and in Chicago it was the South Side. Almost all of those neighborhoods were redlined.[21–24]

Urban Renewal

While many redlined neighborhoods thrived, they were still deemed "slums" or "blighted."[25] These are racially charged terms frequently used to justify the destruction of disinvested neighborhoods. These terms were used in the 1949 American Housing Act and the Federal-Aid Highway Act of 1956, which led to the development of the Interstate Highway System.[25,26]

"To secure political and judicial approval for their efforts, renewal advocates created a new language of urban decline: a discourse of blight," wrote University of Pennsylvania law professor Wendell Pritchett in a 2003 essay "The Public Menace of Blight: Urban Renewal and the Private Uses of Eminent Domain."[27] "Blight, renewal proponents argued, was a disease that threatened to turn healthy areas into slums." During the urban renewal era, between 1950 and 1974, over $13 billion in grants were given to 1,200 municipalities in the United States to redevelop "blighted" areas. "At least half of those cities executed projects that collectively displaced, *at minimum*, a third of a million families," notes the "Renewing Inequality" website, a project of the University of Richmond extending from their project "Mapping Inequality."[28,29] The massive amount of displacement, particularly in the large urban areas, affected predominantly Black and Brown communities.

Civil rights activist and writer James Baldwin's statement that "urban renewal . . . means negro removal" became a rallying cry for protests against displacement.[30] "The federal government is an accomplice of this fact," he said.

"In St. Paul it was the Rondo neighborhood, in Minneapolis it was the 38th and Chicago neighborhood where George Floyd was murdered,"

(a)

(b)

FIGURE 2-2 (a) The San Juan neighborhood of New York in 1956 before the buildings were demolished to build Lincoln Center (Source: Committee on Slum Clearance/Public Domain). (b) Lincoln Center for the Performing Arts in New York in 2019 in what was the San Juan neighborhood. (Photo by Ajay Suresh/Creative Commons License; https://commons.wikimedia.org/w/index.php?curid=79641427)

Heather Worthington says. "So, there's a history of racial violence and disparities that has been well documented in the Twin Cities and in particular in Minneapolis."

These decisions continue to arrest the mobility of Black Americans.

"Redlining created the crisis that urban renewal was created to solve," said Brent Cebul, urban historian at the University of North Carolina, Charlotte, and a co-author of *Renewing Inequality*.[31] In addition to making way for new freeways as a part of the development of the Interstate Highway System, urban renewal made way for development that served higher-income White community members. A prime example is New York's Lincoln Center, now a center of creative arts that caters to the upper class (Figure 2-2b). To make way for Lincoln Center, the city demolished the thriving Black and Latino neighborhood of San Juan Hill (Figure 2-2a).[32]

The Enduring Legacy of Segregation

"Black Americans are twice as likely as White Americans to be struck and killed, and Native Americans are three times as likely . . . to be struck and killed while walking," said Beth Osborne, director of Transportation for America.[33,34]

One reason for the disparity in roadway deaths is that Black and lower-income communities often have high-traffic corridors running through them and are less likely to benefit from investments in safety measures such as traffic calming, well-lit bus stops, well-marked and frequent road crossings, and multimodal transportation. Research by Rebecca Sanders of Safe Streets Researching & Consulting and Robert Schneider, a professor of architecture and urban planning at University of Wisconsin, Milwaukee, shows that Black pedestrians are much more likely to be killed on roadways with four or more lanes than White people.[35] "What that suggests is that those really dangerous roadway characteristics are highly significantly correlated with who lives in an area," Sanders told me on the *Arrested Mobility* podcast. "In other words, where we've put those really dangerous roads is highly significantly correlated with Black neighborhoods."[36]

Beth Osborne explains, "There's so much systemic racism in putting Black and Native Americans in a place where it is harder to afford a vehicle. We know that you don't have the same level of intergenerational wealth because so much of our history obliterated that wealth, especially in terms of property for Black and Native Americans."[37]

In some cases, neighborhoods were designed to keep out non-White people. For example, when the wealthy Guilford neighborhood in Baltimore was designed in 1913–1914 as a Whites-only garden suburb by the Roland Park Company, access was restricted from the neighboring Black communities with dead-end streets.[38,39]

Those physical barriers still exist as an enduring reminder of racist planning decisions. According to the 2017 Baltimore City Neighborhood Health profile, the Guilford neighborhood is still predominantly White (70 percent), and the neighboring communities of The Waverlies and Greater Govans are predominantly Black (76.4 percent and 90.4 percent, respectively).[40] There remains an implicit message that Black neighbors are not welcome in Guilford because little has been done to remove the barriers or to integrate the neighborhoods.

The situation is similar in the Minneapolis lakeside neighborhoods Heather Worthington spoke of that were strictly zoned to be White-only. "When we look at South Minneapolis, those restrictions were set in the early 1900s," she says. "But that segregation pattern persists today, almost 120 years later." As a consequence, the neighborhoods remain predominantly White.[41]

Banning zoning that is exclusively single-family was approved as part of the Minneapolis 2040 plan, but it was blocked by the courts in 2023.[42]

Today, most planning policies and practices are not as overtly racist as they were in the mid-twentieth century. But they rarely take history into account. The displacement of Black and Brown residents continues to occur when no measures, such as land use policies, have been put in place to allow residents to stay in their homes as neighborhoods gentrify.[43]

The laws enacted through public policy, even those with good intentions, can have devastating effects on Black Americans. And we must see their history as being the gears of structural racism.

There are many efforts today to undo the historic effects of zoning laws. Those solutions will be discussed in Chapter 4.

ARRESTED MOBILITY THROUGH LAWS AND PUBLIC POLICY

Enacting and enforcing laws through the "colorblind" approach—meaning race is not considered when passing that law—is a major contributor to arrested mobility in the United States today. Laws that are put into place to improve safety often pose different and potentially more harmful consequences for Black citizens. The next chapter goes into more detail about overpolicing practices. In this chapter I focus on specific mobility types and laws around them, and the planning decisions that lead to behaviors that can be policed (riding on the sidewalk, for example, because there are no bike lanes or safe routes on the road).

Walking While Black

In 2017 *ProPublica* and the *Florida Times-Union* ran a series, "Walking While Black," which showed how Jacksonville, Florida, police used ticketing of pedestrians as a means of overpolicing people of color.[44] The article told the story of John Fitzgerald Kendrick, who was threatened with a taser, commanded to the ground, and charged with jaywalking because he stepped off the sidewalk into the roadway.

Many pedestrian laws are outdated and obscure and don't increase safety. Walking is one of the most fundamental ways of moving through public space, which is regulated by laws at the state and local level that invite discriminatory enforcement. But pedestrian laws haven't always been around.

In her book *Right of Way: Race, Class, and the Silent Epidemic of Pedestrian Deaths in America*, journalist Angie Schmitt highlights the origin of criminalization of walking.[45] Before the 1920s, pedestrian laws didn't exist, but with the proliferation of the Model T Ford, more people were being killed by cars. "So there was a lot of panic and moral outrage about this at the time, and there were groups organizing—particularly groups of mothers who had lost children—who were organizing under the banner of the National Safety Council and cities across the country," Schmitt told me. "In response to that, there was this organized campaign by car dealers, gasoline sellers, they sort of organized and put forward this idea that streets were for cars and that pedestrians shouldn't be in the roadway except in very limited circumstances."[46]

The term *jaywalking* was invented by the car industry to brand pedestrians in a negative light if they didn't follow the pedestrian laws and to support the adoption of the car. (*Jay* was a term for a country bumpkin.) Today, jaywalking laws affect predominantly pedestrians of color. Data collected by *Streetsblog* showed that nearly 90 percent of jaywalking tickets issued in 2019 by the New York Police Department were to Black or Hispanic pedestrians, although the city's Black and Hispanic population was only 55 percent of the total population.[47]

Although the overpolicing of Black drivers has been well studied, the impact of laws regulating Americans traveling by other modes and how Black Americans are disproportionately affected has received less attention. In 2023, my company, Equitable Cities, surveyed policies related to foot, bicycle, and e-scooter travel and their effect on Black Americans in the two largest cities in each state as well as in all fifty states.[48]

Since the adoption of jaywalking laws, there has been a proliferation of laws and policies geared toward protecting drivers instead of protecting pedestrians. Many of these are less common and have drawn less attention from researchers and advocates, such as using the right half of a crosswalk, suddenly leaving the curb, playing ball, pedestrians on highways and freeways, pedestrians soliciting rides, and detention for reasonable cause. These laws, though appearing benign or even beneficial in protecting pedestrians, actually have the result of arresting mobility.

Our arrested mobility scan identified key ways in which twelve laws related to pedestrians disproportionately affect Black communities (Figure 2-3). The takeaway is that many of these laws are highly subjective and con-

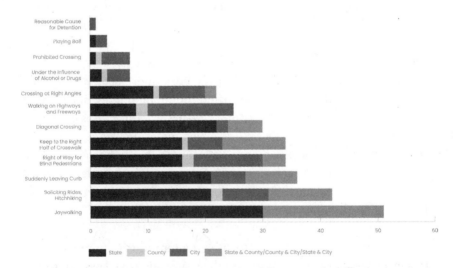

FIGURE 2-3 In our Equitable Cities arrested mobility scan of pedestrian laws in the United States, we found that 100 percent of states have laws that make it illegal to cross outside a crosswalk, 82 percent of states have laws against pedestrians walking on highways, and 60 percent of states have laws against suddenly leaving the curb. (Data visualization by LEFF, leffcommunications.com)

fusing. Many of these pedestrian laws are vaguely worded, such as "suddenly leaving the curb," leading to interpretation and subjective enforcement. The nature of these laws makes equitable enforcement difficult, if not impossible. Laws are enforced more harshly against Black pedestrians, leading to a disproportionate number of citations and encounters with law enforcement that can escalate, resulting in more serious consequences. This vagueness leaves opportunity for discriminatory enforcement. Additionally, there is little evidence that these policies actually improve safety. Instead, they appear to serve as tools of control that maintain racial hierarchies, under the guise of public safety.

These laws "basically delegitimize the right of people to be in the street at all," says Mike McGinn of America Walks. "Is it actually making people safer? And it's actually not walkers and bikers running into people and killing them, it's usually people in vehicles that are doing so. Those are the deadly items on the street."[49]

In neighborhoods where access to private vehicles is limited and infrastructure such as parks and sidewalks is inadequate, residents are more likely to use street space to walk. Therefore, these laws are nearly impossible to enforce equitably.

In recent years, some cities and states have recognized how these laws contribute to racial disparities and have taken steps to address them.

For instance, Virginia decriminalized jaywalking in 2021 as part of broader criminal justice reforms. This change was motivated by the understanding that such laws were often used as pretexts for discriminatory police stops, disproportionately targeting Black pedestrians.[50] And in September 2024, the New York City Council passed a bill revoking the police department's authority to ticket people for jaywalking.[51] These changes will be discussed further in Chapter 4. (Figure 2-4.)

Although some Black citizens may feel less safe walking, biking, or scooting because every move is policed, people such as Michael Kelley, the director of policy at BikeWalkKC, actively seek out the joy of walking as an act of resistance. As a Black man, Kelley admits that he often feels at risk walking on streets that don't have sidewalks because he may be stopped for looking suspicious.

"But that doesn't deter me because I know that as an individual, walking is good for my health, and it's especially important as a Black man to do more to ensure my own health because that is something that is oftentimes

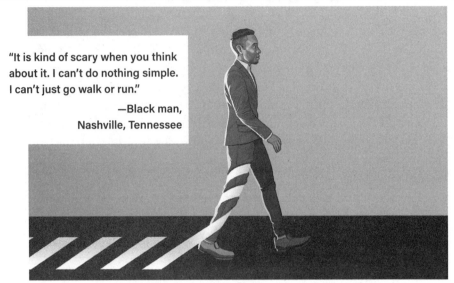

FIGURE 2-4 Walking while Black. (Illustration by Tom Grillo)

one of the first things to be harmed when that infrastructure is removed from us," he says. "Also [I walk] to be an example for my daughters to show them that it is possible in Kansas City but to thrive and to show them what thriving means. It's to show that joy and I take great joy in walking even if I have to have those concerns. Because I know that showing that joy is the only way that I can instill in them that same sense of wonder or that same sense of peace but also that same sense of determination to continue to push for something that is better than what they initially found."[52]

Biking While Black

In January 2017, Patrick McCoy, a seventy-five-year-old Black cyclist from Chicago, was planning to ride his bike to a friend's restaurant. He rolled his bike out of his gate and rode it on the sidewalk to the alley when he was approached by two White police officers. Patrick had no idea why they stopped him. "Because you were riding on the sidewalk," one officer said. "I said, you have got to be kidding me," says McCoy. "Nobody is on the street, it's 15 degrees. And I'm only going less than 50 feet on the sidewalk. He said you know you're not supposed to ride on the sidewalk. I say yes, I know that, but that's not what this is . . . and he said, we could arrest you."[53]

McCoy believes he was stopped to meet a quota. He lives in the South Side near the University of Chicago, which has one of the largest private police forces in the country, and there is a large presence from the Chicago Police Department. "They had to get a certain amount of tickets, and it's easy to do it in a Black neighborhood because you're not gonna get any pushback," says McCoy.[54] Although Illinois banned police ticketing quotas in 2014, only recently have lawmakers introduced a law (HB4976) to remove language that allows the performance of police officers to be evaluated on ticketing.[55] Even if quotas are banned, there may be unspoken assumptions by superiors who expect a certain level of ticketing by officers.

McCoy managed to keep his cool despite attempts by the police to provoke him and left without a ticket or arrest. The law against riding a bike on the sidewalk is technically meant to keep the public safe, but what it really does is make it more dangerous for Black cyclists because it increases the likelihood of encounters with the police.

Although state laws play a role, laws governing bicycling are generally made at the local level, depending on a city's jurisdiction, and are grouped under two categories: riding activities and licensing and equipment (Figure 2-5). Laws governing riding activities include laws prohibiting riding two abreast, carrying articles while cycling, wearing headsets or earplugs, engaging in trick riding or acrobatic riding, speeding, not yielding while emerging

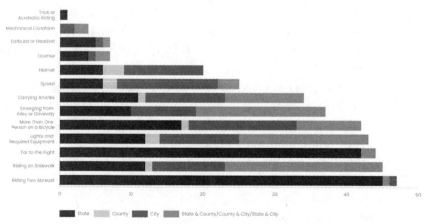

FIGURE 2-5 In our Equitable Cities arrested mobility scan of biking laws, we found that 90 percent of states have laws that forbid riding two abreast or riding far to the right, 64 percent of states have laws against riding on the sidewalk, and 56 percent of states have laws requiring bicycle lights. (Data visualization by LEFF, leffcommunications.com)

from an alley or driveway, carrying anyone other than the operator on your bike, sidewalk riding, and biking anywhere but far to the right. Licensing and equipment laws include possessing a bicycle license, wearing a helmet, being equipped with a bike lamp while riding at night, and maintaining one's bike properly. Helmet laws are the most common reason police stop cyclists under the category of regulating equipment. Additionally, there are laws that allow police to inspect bikes if there's reasonable cause to suspect improper equipment.

In 2021, Jesus M. Barajas, a researcher from the University of California, Davis, analyzed Chicago police citations and found that 90 percent of all bicycle-related infractions were for cycling on the sidewalk.[56] Additionally, he found that Chicago police wrote eight times as many tickets for cycling on the sidewalk in majority Black neighborhoods as in majority White areas and three times as many in Latino areas.[57] His study determined that these tickets were only "weakly associated with safety needs, if at all," raising questions about the value and purpose of the stops.[58]

Barajas found bike infrastructure lacking in the Black communities he studied in Chicago. He said, "The intersection of that lack of infrastructure and the over-policing led to a higher number of bike citations than you might expect if that infrastructure had been present." They looked at biking infrastructure such as bike lanes and bike boulevards and where bikes share routes with vehicles in the city.[59]

Barajas doesn't think that enforcing bicycle laws is a good use of resources. He said, "The role of enforcement should be to protect and improve safety and we don't have a lot of evidence that riding a bike on the sidewalk is a dangerous activity to the extent that it is to other behaviors."[60]

For cyclists such as Patrick McCoy who live in majority Black neighborhoods where there is a lack of infrastructure, the safest option might be to ride on the sidewalk. It's an example of a community with the least investment in traffic safety improvements and an overrepresentation of police presence. This shows that the solutions to make streets safer shouldn't necessarily include more policing, given how inequitably these kinds of laws are enforced.

The lack of infrastructure and potential for increased run-ins with the police could prevent Black people from cycling. Barajas found that between 2016 and 2018, Black cyclists accounted for only 6 percent of bicycle trips.[61] Black cyclists were much more likely to be stopped by police and be involved in accidents, and they accounted for 15 percent of bicycle fatalities.[62]

The Urban Planning Strategies That Have Shaped Our Communities   45

FIGURE 2-6 Biking while Black. (Illustration by Tom Grillo)

In a survey my group conducted in 2017 of cyclists in New Jersey, we found that 15 percent of all respondents were unfairly targeted by the police while cycling.[63] Of that 15 percent of cyclists, the majority identified as Black or mixed race. In the story reporting on this research, *Bicycling* magazine looked at three major cities that collect data on race in cycling stops: Oakland, New Orleans, and Washington, DC. In all three cities, Black riders were stopped disproportionately more than White riders.[64] In New Orleans, eight of the ten areas with bike tickets were in Black and Latinx neighborhoods. In Oakland, Black riders were stopped three times more often than White riders. In Washington, DC, Black cyclists accounted for 88 percent of stops despite being only half the population of the city. (Figure 2-6.)

For people like Patrick McCoy, the laws have fortunately not stopped him from experiencing the delight of riding. It's the freedom that he loves about that mode of transportation.

"The freedom to be able to move through the universe on my own energy and to move beyond the distance that you would normally be able to walk," he says. "In fact, a long time ago [I read an issue of] *Scientific American* on cycling. . . . I don't know if their analysis is still correct, but they identified that a human being on a bicycle was the most energy efficient mode of transportation in the universe, the amount of energy that is required to move that mass that far that fast. There's nothing that compares to it. So, it's just a very exhilarating concept that at this age, I can do this easier than I can walk."[65]

It's stories like McCoy's that show we need to invest in bike infrastructure in Black communities rather than policing how they move about a city.

E-Biking and E-Scooting While Black

One of the newest modes of modern transportation is e-scooters, which have become ubiquitous in urban centers. E-bikes and e-scooters are the most commonly thought of when you hear the term *micromobility*. This is due in large part to e-bike and e-scooter share programs that have proliferated across the United States. Scooter shares are largely dockless, meaning they don't need to be docked at a specific location. Many bike shares have docked systems, but some programs are dockless.

Because of the agility of micromobility vehicles, transportation experts believe that they can serve an important role in transportation equity by addressing the first-and-last-mile problem, which is the lack of connection between someone's destination and public transit. Thus, they can increase the availability and affordability of micromobility in underserved and under-resourced neighborhoods.

However, as the use of micromobility vehicles has increased, so have concerns about safety and nuisance complaints. The US Consumer Product Safety Commission reported that injuries associated with e-bikes and e-scooters increased nearly 21 percent between 2021 and 2022.[66] Public nuisance concerns are largely about riding on the sidewalk and leaving dockless shared e-bikes and e-scooters in the middle of sidewalks, which are hazards and impediments to people with disabilities. Local and regional jurisdictions have responded by implementing laws that, like most of those I've described here, are almost impossible to enforce equitably.

In the Equitable Cities policy scan, we found that not every state has e-scooter laws. Where there are laws, we found that they are centered around license or registration requirements, speed limits, and parking. Data are limited, but there are anecdotes by Black e-scooter users that indicate inequities in enforcement. For example, in 2021 in Miami Beach, Florida, police confronted Dalonta Crudup for an illegally parked scooter, so he quickly scooted away. He was accused of fleeing and assaulting an officer, because the initial encounter began with Crudup accidentally striking an officer with his scooter, but he claimed that he had ridden away out of fear. Police chased Crudup into the hotel where he was staying and beat him, leaving him with a black eye, bruised ribs, and a bloody chin. Khalid Vaughan, a bystander who began recording the incident, was violently assaulted by the cops after they beat Crudup. All four officers have been relieved of duty.[67] In 2020, in Beverly Hills, California, Khalil White and his partner, Jasmine Williams, were detained and spent the night in jail for riding scooters on the sidewalk and resisting arrest. They saw no signs stating they could not ride on the sidewalk. In response, they filed a lawsuit alleging racial profiling.[68]

Communities are regulating e-scooters by using the same sidewalk riding laws that are an issue for bike riders. Other cities are regulating scooters with speed limits and "geofencing," a technology built into the scooters that automatically slows them down in certain places (although it doesn't always work well), raising similar problems with inequitable enforcement of the law.

Ashley Scott, who served as the public policy director for the e-scooter company Lime until 2022, said that access to micromobility vehicles is bringing in new riders who aren't as aware of riding etiquette, and so there's a learning curve around the laws. "What we're seeing is that people are engaging in things like sidewalk riding, but I think what it leads to is a greater conversation about where a rider feels safe to ride," she says.[69]

Some cities in which Lime operated asked the company to detect when riders were riding on the sidewalk, issue them a fine, and remove them from the platform if they were repeat offenders. As a Black woman, Scott is aware of the inequity involved in that approach.

Scott grew up in the historically Black neighborhood of Liberty City in south Florida. "There aren't many consistent sidewalks, but when there are, they usually are busy cross sections of the street so my natural inclination may be to ride on the sidewalk," she says. "So, if Lime then offers scooters in that area, and I ride and have been detected . . . on the sidewalk 234 times and the city now wants to remove me from the platform. What you're doing is causing a domino effect of victimizing low-income riders or riders that primarily traverse underserved areas that do not have protected bike lanes or shared paths."[70]

She knows that it's not the intention of the city to victimize low-income community members and that they're trying to "keep a pulse on concerns from the disability rights community," she says. "But they are now taking antiquated laws and enforcement and privatizing it."[71]

Steve Wright, disability rights advocate and professor of universal design at the University of Miami School of Architecture, believes that there can be a middle-ground solution. "It's an interim and if we . . . make a strong case for infrastructure that's humane . . . we can have a very wide sidewalk and we can have a bike lane and we can have some sort of marked lane for the scooters," he says. "The idea that this is weaponized . . . the idea that a Brown or Black person has maybe had a 50/50 chance of getting a ticket or being called over and read the riot act . . . that's not a world that I want to live in."[72]

The laws can't be enforced equitably when the residents of communities with the least public investment must break those laws more in order to move around their community.

ARRESTED MOBILITY AND THE PROFESSION OF URBAN PLANNING AND DESIGN

There tends to be an assumption by urban planners and engineers that as long as there are good intentions now, the historic wrongs perpetuated by our fields don't need to be considered. There has been considerable movement by planners and engineers to ensure we don't make the same mistakes, but progress has been slow. The American Institute of Certified Planners code of ethics addresses economic, social, and racial equity; however, the code is presented as a goal.[73] There are no requirements for planners to learn how to take an equity approach and do it well. It is no surprise that White norms are baked into urban and regional planning, given that over 75 percent of planners were White as of 2022 and only 5.88 percent of planners were Black.[74] There has been a slight increase in diversity over the years, including having Black presidents at the helm of the American Planning Association, but it's clear that the field has a long way to go before there is true representation.

I conducted a survey of Black scholars in transportation, public health, and land use, and they reflected back the slow progress in diversifying the field, which they believe is because it's so hard for their White colleagues to truly understand the mechanism of systemic racism. The actions needed to dismantle these systems have not been discussed or acted on in a meaningful way.

One participant stated that their White counterparts can see how things are racist, but they do not understand the various layers and interconnectedness of it all.[75] And this is reflected in the way cities are designed through the lens of White-dominant culture.

Veronica O. Davis puts a fine point on this in her book *Inclusive Transportation: A Manifesto for Repairing Divided Communities*. "When the dominant culture is centered on you, it becomes easy to assume that someone else's experience is the same as yours," she writes. "If you are a White man, it becomes easy not to notice that the entire leadership of your company is mostly White men. If you are able-bodied, it becomes easy to say 'Remove a bus stop to speed up the buses; walking two extra blocks is not a big deal.'"[76]

Who Has Agency?

Black and Brown neighborhoods continue to be ignored even when city and regional planning entities claim to be dedicated to improving *all* parts of a community. We have yet to undo the policies and practices that created harm in the first place. Heather Worthington says, "There is a kind of issue around agency when it comes to your ability to access that elected official that I think is kind of subtle and not well understood. White homeowners never are unclear about this. They just pick up the phone and call their council members. But I found as we talk to members of cultural communities, and in particular members of the Black community, I heard consistently: *We don't feel like we have a voice at City Hall, I don't feel like I can call my council member, I'm not even sure I know who my council member is*."[77]

Real change could be made with some agency. Smart Growth America's 2022 "Dangerous by Design" report found that 67 percent of fatalities were occurring on 15 percent of the roadways.[78] Beth Osborne said, "If we got serious, we could fix 15% of roadways in no time. In five years, we could make a huge dent in 15% of roadways, and we could go from the embarrassment of the Western world, to, you know at least middle of the pack, if not an incredible turnaround story that everyone points to everywhere."[79]

Crime Prevention Through Environmental Design

We have agency to use many tools at our disposal, but we need to be certain that these tools won't harm communities, as some resulted in arresting Black mobility. For example, in the 1970s, crime prevention through environmental design (CPTED) was developed as a way to alter the built environment to increase human safety.[80] The National Institute of Crime Prevention defines CPTED as "a strategy that brings together community members to examine how an area's physical design can influence human behavior, reduce crime, fear of crime, and improve quality of life. CPTED uses various tools to evaluate environmental conditions and utilize intervention methods to improve space and how it is used."[81] The goal is to create a sense of safety, but safety for whom? CPTED has elements of surveillance, meaning structures are designed to have visibility of the street, good lighting, controlled access to the space, and reinforcement of the space.

"While CPTED principles are said to help discourage crime by orienting building windows and entrances to aid in providing 'eyes on the street' that monitor activity, in practice this strategy can end up serving the same suppressive purpose as stop-and-frisk policing—to assure that anyone considered suspicious is made to feel uncomfortable," wrote Bryan Lee Jr. in *Bloomberg CityLab*.[82] "The problem is when you are black in this country, you live daily with the heavy weight of the world's distrust on your shoulders. In a city like Minneapolis, whose police officers used force against black people at a rate at least seven times that of white residents, such design practices could help create the very conditions that led to Mr. Floyd's murder."[83]

Minneapolis, a city at the center of the racial justice uprising in the wake of George Floyd's murder, has used CPTED in their approach to design. In 2019, the city approved an extension of their CPTED program. What Lee is describing are the early iterations, the first generation of the CPTED model that fell into to the surveillance-heavy category. To a White person, whether a resident of the building or a passerby, the CPTED design evokes a feeling of safety and security. You walk through the space taking for granted that your White skin won't call any attention to you. Of course, that space might make a woman walking alone feel safer. So there are merits to the design elements. But for a Black person, walking at night through a space with delineated access, under illuminated lights, with large windows pointing in that direction, it would be very clear that space is not for them.

I agree with the critics of the first-generation CPTED model that these design elements didn't consider the safety of Black and Brown people. In fact, the term *illegitimate users*, code for Black and Brown people, was often included to describe whom the design was meant to deter from a space.

It's important to recognize that Black people also want safe communities, and CPTED has evolved to include more diverse perspectives that led to an evolution of the model. In fact, I became certified in CPTED in order to bring my perspective as a Black planner to the table. I saw the potential but wanted the approach to consider race and ethnicity more deeply.

The more recent generations of CPTED include values of social cohesion, community culture and connectivity, universal design, gender-sensitive design, age-friendly spaces, and economic inclusivity. These values help to create a community where belonging and trust are centered, which actually reduces crime, unlike a surveillance model.

Design Bias

Designing for the safety of all residents is an exceptionally underresearched area of transportation planning. There are a few details that we do know.

"We know that 3/4 of pedestrian deaths happen during low-light hours and that Black and Latino pedestrians are killed at higher rates," wrote Marisa DeMull, now a senior engineering associate at the Portland Bureau of Transportation in the 2018 article "It's Time for Transportation Engineers to Address Racial Equity."[84] "Are we applying the existing knowledge of how to light dark skin so it's visible at night? Or are we assuming that the code around lighting pedestrians applies to everyone equally?"

DeMull later wrote, "At this time there are no studies that show the (obvious) correlation between race and lighting."[85] But she argues the potential for engineers to think creatively and perhaps look at other professions where there might actually be research, specifically photography. "We have a multitude of evidence from studies, starting in the 1960s with ophthalmology research, that investigate lighting types (high pressure sodium, LED) and lighting levels," she wrote. "Many studies zero in on dark objects, most especially dark colored clothing, and how they impact drivers' ability to see pedestrians."

She acknowledges that lighting is something considered by transportation engineers. "In fact we actually include in our model for lighting design a reflectance level to account for dark colored clothing, black asphalt and soil (all of which have a low reflectance rate)—and yet no one has designed a study to look at the reflectance of dark skin."

The lack of research shows that there's a missing piece in the way we design our buildings and streets. This happens when the White-dominant culture is the status quo and goes unquestioned.

In response, architects and planners such as Bryan Lee Jr. are taking a design justice approach. "Design Justice seeks to dismantle the privilege and power structures that use architecture as a tool of oppression and sees it as an opportunity to envision radically just spaces centered on the liberation of disinherited communities," he wrote.[86] (I'll go into more detail about solutions like design justice in Chapters 4 and 5.)

There is still a long way to go before all spaces are designed for the safety of all people.

My hope is that understanding how urban planning and policy have shaped a society that has arrested the mobility of Black Americans will open our eyes to where change and correction are desperately needed. Planners and policymakers must recognize that their actions, however well intentioned, might not always lead to the intended outcome of safety. In fact, these actions may often cause significant harm.

It's crucial that we begin to see our work through this lens, acknowledging the possibility that our solutions could perpetuate inequities rather than resolve them. This shift in perspective is essential for driving the change we need in our communities.

I also hope that academics in urban planning will have the courage to deeply explore the role of race in shaping the built environment and its impact on arrested mobility for Black communities. It is vital that they teach their students—the future planners of our cities—not just the technical skills of planning but also how race and systemic racism influence the spaces we create. They should be inspired by scholars such as Dr. Deadric Williams, who emphasize the importance of addressing the root causes of racial disparities rather than merely treating their symptoms.[87]

By fostering a deeper understanding of these dynamics, we can transform planners and policymakers into advocates for true equity rather than allowing them to unknowingly perpetuate chaos and harm. This is not just about doing better work; it's about fulfilling a moral responsibility to create safe, just, and equitable communities for all.

THREE

Policing

The Means by Which Unequal Systems Are Reinforced

"It is a peculiar sensation, this double-consciousness, this sense of always looking at one's self through the eyes of others."
—W. E. B. Du Bois, *The Souls of Black Folk*

"Violence for White people really has too often had a Black face—and the consequences have landed on the Black body across the span of American history."
—Ibram X. Kendi, *How to Be an Antiracist*

When my son was about seven years old, we were walking in downtown Somerville, New Jersey, with our friends, another dad and son, both White. My son's White friend took off running down the sidewalk with as much freedom to be young and playful as any kid should have. My son, clearly wanting to join his buddy, hesitated and then looked back at me. I could tell his first assumption was that he wasn't allowed to run like his friend. It was instinct that made him turn to me.

I gave him permission to run alongside his friend, but that moment hit me, especially in direct contrast to the experience of our White friends. I felt our Blackness in that public space. While my son was looking to me for permission, we both knew deep down, it was how we were perceived by the people around us that would determine our safety and acceptance in that public space.

When he ran off, I felt conflicted. I was deeply saddened that he felt the need to ask permission, that he couldn't live his life freely like his White friend. And I was anxious, looking around at the people around them wondering whether they would be a threat to my son because all they saw was his Blackness.

What often leads children like my son to be more cautious is what we in Black culture call "The Talk." The Talk is the conversation parents and caregivers have with their young Black children about how the world (especially law enforcement) perceives them.

I cannot remember the first time that I was given The Talk or the first time that I gave it to my son. The Talk was embedded in the way my mother said goodbye—*I love you, be careful*—leaving me last with her warning of what was outside. I heard or gave The Talk so many times that whenever I leave the house, I feel like I'm looking out for my survival and keeping my eyes open to threats to my Black body. When I think about the intergenerational trauma of having one's mobility arrested, I think of The Talk. The Talk makes it painfully clear that Black people have been "othered," and we are traveling a completely different road than our White peers.

With every Black American killed by police or a self-deputized White citizen, we're viscerally reminded of the very thin line for Black Americans to break the perceived social code.

In the wake of the murder of George Floyd, Kenya Young, executive producer of the NPR podcast *It's Been a Minute*, talked about her experience as a mother of three Black sons.[1] She recalled having The Talk with her kids soon after Philando Castile and Alton Sterling were murdered by the police.

"I remember the kids asking to go to the park and the laundry list of what I had to tell them," she says. "'Don't wear your hood. Don't put your hands in your pocket. If you get stopped, don't run. Put your hands up. Don't make a lot of moves. Tell them your mother works for *NPR*.' I mean, it just went on and on."[2]

The Talk has become such an embedded part of the Black experience in the United States because police encounters are much more deadly for Black Americans than White Americans. (Figure 3-1.)

FIGURE 3-1 Even young Black children have to receive "The Talk" because of the way society and the police view them as dangerous. (Illustration by Katrina Kopeloff of Illustrating Progress, 2023)

Research has found that Black and Latino drivers are stopped disproportionately more than White drivers, and after the stop Black and Latino drivers are much more likely to be searched than White drivers.[3] According to the Pew Research Center, Black adults are five times more likely to say that they've been unfairly stopped by the police.[4] According to a 2020 study from the Stanford Open Policing Project, Black drivers are less likely to carry guns, drugs, or illegal contraband than White drivers, yet they are 20 percent more likely to be stopped by police than White drivers and are searched 1.5 to 2 times more often.[5]

In Minnesota, a 2016 state-commissioned study found that in White majority neighborhoods, Blacks and Latinos were seven times more likely to be stopped by police.[6] In the suburbs of St. Paul, Minnesota, the St. Anthony police released data after Philando Castile was pulled over, shot, and killed by police in July 2016. "About 7 percent of the residents in the area patrolled are African-American, but this year they make up about 47 percent of arrests," wrote Eyder Peralta and Cheryl Corley about an *NPR* analysis. "The data show that since 2011, African-Americans have been making up a larger percentage of arrests."[7] These data track nationally. According to Ronnie Dunn, associate professor of urban studies at Cleveland State University, Black drivers are 2.5 times more likely to receive a traffic ticket than White drivers.[8]

According to the website Mapping Police Violence, 10 percent of police killings start with traffic stops.[9] In a country where Black people are three times as likely to be killed by police as White people, the risk to Black drivers is much greater with every traffic stop.[10]

Police often use minor traffic violations as a justification to investigate unrelated crimes without a warrant. This is known as a pretextual stop, because an officer identifies a violation of a traffic code as a pretext to "investigate a hunch that, by itself, would not amount to reasonable suspicion or probable cause," as law professors Stephen Rushin and Griffin Edwards wrote in 2022.[11]

Being overpoliced in traffic stops not only is dangerous for Black Americans but puts an undue financial burden on them. *Vox* writer Marin Cogan describes how cars fuel racial inequality.[12] She tells the story of Leisa Moseley-Sayles, who moved to Las Vegas, where an officer issued her a $299 ticket for expired California plates. She wasn't able to keep up on regular payments on the ticket. After missing one payment, she learned that there was a warrant for her arrest unless she paid the remaining amount on the ticket and an additional $150 fine. Late fees accumulated, and eventually she was pulled over again. The officer then suspended her license.

Cogan explains that this story isn't unique. "As of 2021, about 11 million Americans had their driver's licenses suspended due to nonpayment of fines and fees. It took Moseley-Sayles nearly a decade—by which time she'd paid off her initial ticket plus an additional $5,000 in warrant fees and other fines—to get her license reinstated."[13]

A 2016 study by the Lawyer's Committee for Civil Rights of the San Francisco Bay Area found that driver's license suspensions in Black and Latino communities are five times higher than the California state average.[14] Additionally, Black drivers are much more likely to be driving with a suspended license due to failure to pay a citation.[15]

Before Philando Castile was killed by police, write Peralta and Corley, he "was stopped by police 46 times and racked up more than $6,000 in fines. Another curious statistic: Of all of the stops, only six of them were things a police officer would notice from outside a car—things like speeding or having a broken muffler."[16]

Outside the car, Black and Brown people are also more vulnerable than White people.

New York City's stop-and-frisk data show that 90 percent of the people stopped between 2003 and 2023 were people of color, 52 percent of stops were of Black New Yorkers, and 31 percent were Latinx.[17]

With every stop—whether driving, walking, biking, or scooting—a Black person is at a higher risk of facing police violence or death. The website Mapping Police Violence reports that police kill Black people at a rate 2.9 times higher than White people.[18]

Despite calls for reform, the number of people killed by police rose every year since 2019 and reached an all-time high of 1,353 in 2023.[19] The *Washington Post* reported that fatal police shootings between 2005 and May 2024 were two and a half times more likely to have Black victims than White victims.[20]

Black and White Americans exist in two different worlds when it comes to policing. White people don't have an equivalent to The Talk about dangers based on their race.

POLICING AND MY FAMILY HISTORY

On February 22, 1959, in my hometown of Shuqualak, Mississippi, Nelse and Ella Gaston, my distant relatives, were pulled over by a police vehicle. Quickly they were "surrounded by white men with badges, guns, nightsticks, and nasty attitudes," wrote Pam Johnson in a book about the event and its aftermath called *Justice for Ella: A Story that Needed to Be Told*.[21]

The officers dragged Nelse out of the car to an out-of-sight spot and beat him. They searched the car where his wife, Ella, and two children sat in horror, hacking open the trunk to find, of course, nothing. Ella stepped out of the car to ask the officers to stop beating her husband. The officers reacted by slamming her head and face into the car. Ella and Nelse were taken to the notorious Noxubee County Jail—having done nothing other than driving while Black—leaving their small children in the back of the vehicle. Ella was later convicted of "intimidating an officer."

"The jail, though lovely from the outside, was rotten on the inside. This Nelse knew," wrote Johnson. "He'd been told tales of what happened inside those beautiful brick walls all his life. It wasn't good for anybody, but it was awful for black men and rumored to be worse than that for black women."[22]

Nelse and Ella were released the next day. Ella never disclosed what happened during her night in confinement, but it was deeply traumatizing. It led to Ella and her friend Jewell McMahon fighting to get Ella's conviction overturned by the Mississippi Supreme Court.

It's a story that has found its way into my bones. As a family member, I see Ella and Nelse's story as my story. And in a lot of ways, their story is that of all Black people in the United States. Police officers today may not be as boldly and outwardly racist as those in the Jim Crow South, but the stories of Black Americans intimidated and harmed by police while trying to go about everyday activities is something we all carry.

It's worth noting that I haven't always carried a suspicion of police. It has come about through a lifetime of experiences with law enforcement. Although the system urgently needs to be changed, I still respect law enforcement. If you asked me as a kindergartener what I wanted to be when I grew up, I would answer, "head of the FBI." I have close friends and family members who are law enforcement officers, and I wanted to work in the top tier, even joining the military—which many of them also did—to potentially pursue a career in enforcement. But as I grew up and started to read profusely, I learned about the FBI's alleged murder of Fred Hampton, deputy chairman of the Black Panthers, and the FBI's targeted surveillance of Black Americans, specifically of Civil Rights activists, I changed course.

I also know that members of law enforcement, including some of my family members, want to change the system. I followed a path toward the military where I served our country and respect all who put their lives on the line. But I believe that policies and policing shouldn't be designed with a focus on surveillance. I bring a respect but also, as a Black American, a way of thinking about policing that might differ from that of White Americans.

In mainstream White America, police officers are revered and respected almost by default. Considered "keepers of the peace," the police are often regarded as an essential fixture in the civilized world. This is probably the case for many White people and other people of privilege in this country because the police force does, indeed, protect them. It is another story for Black Americans. Ella and Nelse's story is one of many. This difference in experiences with the police is no surprise when we consider the origins of policing in America.

Policing in the United States exists very much within the Eurocentric capitalist model that was brought here by colonists and imposed as a system of "maintaining order."

POLICING AND SLAVERY

According to Gary Potter, the late crime historian and professor emeritus from Eastern Kentucky University, "maintaining order" in the early years of the United States was done at the community level through community watches.[23] As towns grew in the North, this evolved into a constable system where law enforcement officers were paid by the number of warrants they issued.

"More than crime, modern police forces in the United States emerged as a response to 'disorder,'" wrote Potter.[24] What constituted "disorder" was largely decided by the elites who feared that "disorderly conduct" affected their business and mercantile interests. "These economic interests had a greater interest in social control than crime control."[25]

In the South slavery was still legal and remained an economic driver for the entire country. There was a direct line between the police force and "slave patrols" in the South. Slave patrols were created to track down enslaved people who ran away, discipline enslaved people, and terrorize them to discourage revolts. After the Civil War these vigilante organizations morphed into modern police departments of the South, which created a system of control of formerly enslaved people.

The police forces in the South were notorious for the particularly brutal enforcement of Jim Crow laws. Segregation and the extreme overpolicing of Black Americans are part of the reason that six million Black Americans moved from the Southern states to Northern states between 1910 and 1970.

Known as the Great Migration, it is one of the largest mass migrations of people in US history.[26]

In the Northern states, racism was also embedded in the police force, although it was less overt than in the South.

Planner and mobility justice expert tamika l. butler, who identifies as an abolitionist, has dedicated her career to finding ways to extract the police from traffic and mobility enforcement. "We always have to ask ourselves if keeping vulnerable road users safe is something that police have accomplished," she told me. "I would argue that since the inception of police, to catch and track down runaway slaves, police have not been concerned with vulnerable road users. Instead, they have been part of a power structure aimed at harming and controlling the movement of the most vulnerable."

Policing in America was more about social control than preventing crime. "Defining social control as crime control was accomplished by raising the specter of the 'dangerous classes,'" writes Potter.[27] "The suggestion was that public drunkenness, crime, hooliganism, political protests and worker 'riots' were the products of a biologically inferior, morally intemperate, unskilled and uneducated underclass." Police conspired with politicians to ensure that their political and economic interests were protected. Potter describes the primary characteristics of early police departments: "They were notoriously corrupt and flagrantly brutal. This should come as no surprise in that police were under the control of local politicians."[28]

This created a system that targeted primarily lower-income communities, immigrants, people of color, and any kind of social protest from lower classes to fight for rights, including organized labor and racial justice.

There is, of course, a hierarchy of class system, one that Isabel Wilkerson wrote about poignantly in *Caste: The Origins of Our Discontents*.[29] Using terminology and concepts from India that created a hierarchical system of stratification, she sees caste as undergirding our society.

"The word *caste* is a reminder of an infrastructure beneath something that's larger," she said in a *PBS* interview about her book.[30] "It's something that is the foundation, the framework with how people interact with one another. So I have come to believe that caste, the infrastructure, the hierarchies that we often don't see, are the bones of a thing. I think of caste as the bones and race as the skin. And that is a way to see that race has been used historically as the cue, the signal, the indicator of where an individual fits into the preexisting hierarchy that's been created from the time of colonial era America."

When the role of the police force was used to control the "dangerous classes," race was used as one of the most obvious indicators. The police forces were founded on historical and racial biases.

Mike McGinn from America Walks says, "The police are very often doing exactly what communities are demanding of them." They'll respond to calls of "suspicious people." "And that very often is either a person who appears to be homeless, so they appear to be of very low social standing and means, or they're a young Black person or an Asian male, something that says to the person complaining that, 'They don't belong here, this community is not for them, and I need to get the police there to enforce that.'"[31] Thus, the police are enacting social control as handed down by folks who have power, essentially White people. By assuming police exist as a neutral entity, we are complicit in the harms that come from that enforcement. Involving the police is not a benign act. As a 2023 Pew Research Center poll found, 67 percent of Black people believe the receive less fair treatment by police than White people.[32]

Potter explained that we're seeing this bias continue to play out with technological innovations in policing. "As we look to the 21st century, it now appears likely that a new emphasis on science and technology, particularly related to citizen surveillance; a new wave of militarization reflected in the spread of SWAT teams and other paramilitary squads; and a new emphasis on community pacification through community policing, are all destined to replay the failures of history as the policies of the future."[33]

TRAFFIC SAFETY AND OVERPOLICING

"Right now, lots of money goes from the federal government to states for safety programs . . . [and] a lot of that money for safety goes to police enforcement," says McGinn.[34] "And this idea that enforcement automatically leads to safety is very much an unexamined assumption. . . . It's one of those things that people say, 'Well, it just stands to reason, right? If you have rules, you have to enforce rules.'"

On the *Arrested Mobility* podcast I asked Olatunji Oboi Reed, the president and CEO of Equiticity, which aims to operationalize racial equity

FIGURE 3-2 Interactions with police feel almost inevitable, no matter what form of transportation a Black person takes. (Illustration by Katrina Kopeloff of Illustrating Progress, 2023)

through transformative legislation and policy, whether he thinks law enforcement can play a role in traffic safety.

"Not today," he said. "Policing in our society has a direct line to the institution of slave catchers. And coming out of slavery, and for generations having that foundation is why these systems, these institutions are criminalizing our neighborhoods, and worse, killing us. . . . I don't see a contemporary role for police in improving traffic safety."[35]

I don't believe that policing should be involved in issues of mobility in most circumstances. When we think about the disproportionate enforcement of Black citizens, we shouldn't be using mobility solutions that require law enforcement. (Figure 3-2.)

Over the past two decades, the campaign to end traffic fatalities, Vision Zero, has become integrated in many municipal transportation planning offices. The goal is noble: "eliminate all traffic fatalities and severe injuries, while increasing safe, healthy, and equitable mobility for all."[36]

In addition to elements such as design and education, enforcement is an important part of most Vision Zero campaigns. The Vision Zero approach often has an overreliance on surveillance around speed limits.

This is the major sticking point for people such as Dara Baldwin, director of national policy at the Center for Disability Rights, who clearly sees the link between policing and surveillance to the American history of the enslavement of Black people.

"Those algorithms are created by White men and it's based on law enforcement," she told me. She's wary of any kind of design that seemingly takes a "colorblind" approach, meaning it's more likely that it's not taking into account how Black Americans are treated much more harshly through police enforcement.

Baldwin wants to see programs that are less focused on "fixing people" through punitive approaches and more community-oriented design improvements that compel people to drive safely. Vision Zero has a strong design component, and for the concept to work, there must be a concerted racial equity approach that involves listening to and learning from Black people about what they want in their neighborhood to improve traffic safety. As Beth Osborne said, cities need to be involved in improving the most dangerous roads, which are often in Black and Brown neighborhoods. Cities signing on to Vision Zero should look at solutions in terms of racial equity.

Planners and engineers must think more critically about how streets can be safer without relying on police enforcement (more about this in Chapter 5).

A NEW ERA OF OVERPOLICING

In 2022, twenty-nine-year-old transportation analyst Randal Quran Reid was pulled over in Atlanta and arrested because there were warrants out for his arrest in Louisiana, a state in which he had never set foot. He wasn't told what he was accused of while he was detained for six days. He missed a week of work and was out hundreds of dollars in legal fees for a crime he didn't commit. How did Reid, who is Black, end up in this situation?

"Mr. Reid's wrongful arrest appears to be the result of a cascade of technologies—beginning with a bad facial recognition match—that are intended to make policing more effective and efficient but can also make it far too easy to apprehend the wrong person for a crime," wrote journalists Kashmir Hill and Ryan Mac.[37] What's more, the fact that the accusation came from facial recognition technology was never mentioned to Reid or his family. "Law enforcement officers generally say they do not need to mention the use of facial recognition technology because it is only a lead in a case and not the sole reason for someone's arrest, protecting it from exposure as if it were a confidential informant," they wrote.

Faulty facial recognition technology is an example of how emerging technologies can arrest the mobility of Black Americans. Researchers from Georgia State University found that these technologies are, in fact, increasing racial disparities in arrests.[38] "We found that law enforcement agencies that use automated facial recognition disproportionately arrest Black people," wrote members of the research team, Thaddeus L. Johnson and Natasha N. Johnson.[39] "We believe this results from factors that include the lack of Black faces in the algorithms' training data sets, a belief that these programs are infallible and a tendency of officers' own biases to magnify these issues."

This kind of overreliance on technology is troubling, to say the least, causing newfound concerns about overpolicing of Black Americans. A 2022 *Forbes* article, "The 5 Biggest Tech Trends in Policing and Law Enforcement," evokes a sense of a dystopian future of inequity perpetuated through heightened digital surveillance.[40] One entry on the list is computer vision, which includes license plate and facial recognition technology and access to smart device data such as video doorbells and voice assistants. The story's optimistic tone feels out of sync with the reality of situations for Black people such as Randal Quran Reid. "These technologies give police officers and intelligence agencies unprecedented powers to crack down on criminal activity as they attempt to keep us safe," writes author Bernard Marr.

The potential for video doorbells to increase racial profiling has led some publications such as *Wired* to take a stance against the use of the Amazon brand of cameras, Ring. "We occasionally end up with products that can be dangerous to you, or to society in general, which we believe to be the case with Amazon-owned Ring and its relationship with law enforcement," wrote Adrienne So, *Wired* senior associate reviews editor.[41] So notes that their Gears team has been concerned about vigilante surveillance with the introduction of these devices. "It makes it easier for both private citizens and law enforcement agencies to target certain groups for suspicion of crime based on skin color, ethnicity, religion, or country of origin," she wrote. The Ring's direct line of contact to law enforcement is a "frictionless feature" that makes it too easy for a "concerned" neighbor to call the police on someone.[42]

Amazon has only made it easier for citizens to police others by partnering with police departments to hand out free devices to people in a community through the Neighbors Public Safety Service.[43]

MIT researchers call this use of door cams "participatory mass surveillance."[44] Although research on racial profiling and doorbell cameras is yet to emerge, there is plenty of anecdotal evidence that shows how they arrest the mobility of Black Americans.

Do these doorbell cameras actually make a community safer? The MIT Media Lab conducted the first nationwide survey of Ring users that asked this question.[45] Analyzing the data in Los Angeles showed that there was little impact on crime, if any.[46]

The prevalence of surveillance mechanisms paired with the embedded internalized racism within society has made Black people less safe.

THE TOLL OF OVERPOLICING

It pains me to have to talk to my own child about what *he* must do to make other people feel safe so that he doesn't become another name added to the rolls of Black Americans taken too soon. The responsibility should not be on him but on society to change. That constant threat takes its toll on mental health.

In a 2014 study, Columbia University researchers found that greater interaction with the police was inextricably linked with increased anxiety and with even more intrusive forms of policing (e.g., entering the home, policing that included body searches or physical encounters), which are linked to a heightened sense of trauma and anxiety, including posttraumatic stress disorder (PTSD).[47] The study also found that PTSD was much more common among Black respondents.[48]

In 2020, researchers Jordan DeVylder, Lisa Fedina, and Bruce Link[49] published a theoretical framework that shows police violence and overpolicing of Black and Brown communities affect mental health and are public health issues.[50] The framework distinguishes police violence from other types of violence. "Police organizations in the United States are . . . authoritative institutions legitimized to apply force—and potentially fatal force—to maintain a particular social and political order," the authors state. "In interactions with civilians, police officers are in positions of relatively greater power because of both the symbolic and state-sanctioned status of their profession, and their immediate legal availability of means (e.g., guns, batons, tasers) to wield force, threat of force, and coercion, at their discretion. This distinguishes police violence from interpersonal forms of violence that are perpetrated by people who are not sanctioned to enact violence, such as caregivers, peers, or intimate partners."[51]

Police are often allowed to use any means necessary with impunity. Many people have died at the hands of police without convictions or even charges filed against the officers. If goals to "maintain safety" involve the police, we must consider what it means for the safety of Black, Brown, and other historically marginalized people.

The higher incarceration rate of Black people in the United States, addressed in Chapter 2, takes a toll on individuals, families, and communities. In the Sentencing Project's 2021 report "The Color of Justice: Racial and Ethnic Disparity in State Prisons," author Ashley Nellis explains, "The presence of a criminal record that results from an arrest or conviction is associated with the decision to incarcerate for subsequent offenses, a sequence of events that disadvantages African Americans."[52] It's a cycle that repeats itself and therefore has an enormous negative impact on Black communities. Incarceration makes it much harder to get a job and to find stable housing once you're released and reduces a person's lifetime earnings, putting formerly incarcerated people into precarious financial positions for the rest of their lives. And on the societal level, Nellis writes, "high levels of imprisonment in communities cause high crime rates and neighborhood deterioration, thus fueling greater disparities."

The work of planners and transportation professionals is interconnected with the role of the police in our communities.

No matter what our role is, we need to consider the impacts of our work on the people who use public spaces. The system is designed by and for White people, yet there's an assumption that the decisions we make in planning and design are neutral. They rarely are.

The first step is understanding the history, and the next step is to consider the implications of all design and planning decisions, particularly through the lens of Black Americans.

FOUR

Un-Arresting Mobility

What It Will Take to Solve Inequity in Mobility

"It is certain, in any case, that ignorance, allied with power, is the most ferocious enemy justice can have."
—James Baldwin

"White Americans must recognize that justice for black people cannot be achieved without radical changes in the structure of our society."
—Dr. Martin Luther King Jr.,
Where Do We Go From Here, 1967

When I left Shuqualak, I heard stories from other communities across the country that were harmed by urban planning. What I didn't see were people who looked like me who had answers to why we lacked a quality grocery store, why the state highway destroyed our community, and why White flight led to economic decline, housing devaluation, education inequality, and concentrated poverty. I felt like I could do something to change that. What that turned into was becoming an urban planner and truth seeker.

I often feel disheartened by how the planning profession continues to reinforce inequities in our system, but I'm optimistic because I see there are solutions that are thoroughly within our grasp when it comes to un-arresting mobility. It will take a concerted effort, particularly among leaders who are not Black, to see potential solutions through the experiences of Black Americans. I am not advocating for a savior but for allies and accomplices.

Veronica Davis writes, "The word 'equity' has lost its meaning among planners and engineers. It has been reduced to a map or an analysis."[1] To ensure that *equity* has meaning in our work, we must actively work to un-arrest the mobility of Black Americans.

Un-arresting mobility involves deemphasizing enforcement, rethinking how we design and invest in our communities, and acknowledging the role of systemic racism in urban planning, policymaking, and the policing of our communities. By reframing how laws are made, encouraging and promoting planning through a racial equity framework, and rethinking policing in America, we can create safe spaces for all people.

This chapter provides snapshots of changes that are already happening to show that it is possible. The next chapter provides detailed solutions through the lens of four change-makers working on equity in mobility.

REPEALING OR REFRAMING ROAD SAFETY LAWS

A major solution to reframing road safety solutions is to *decriminalize mobility*. Because criminalizing behaviors around mobility has made roads less safe for Black people, and laws that criminalize behaviors of pedestrians, bicyclists, and people on scooters have not achieved the goal of increasing safety and lead to racially discriminatory enforcement, they need to be repealed. Violations need to be decriminalized and alternative, fair enforcement must be promoted for policies that affect safety. This includes the decriminalization of minor traffic violations.

In 2022, Philadelphia became the first city in the United States to ban police stops for minor traffic violations, such as a broken brake light or expired registration, after data showed these stops overwhelmingly targeted Black drivers.[2] While racial disparities remained, a year after the ban, traffic stops involving Black men were down 54 percent.[3] Philadelphia police were making 70 percent fewer stops overall, but more traffic stops resulted in a recovery of a gun than they did in 2019, before the ban went into effect.[4] "While there are too many variables to exclusively credit the law for this change," writes Sam Raim for *Vera*, "the results are consistent with the notion that eliminating these low-level stops forces police to be more intentional with their serves and contradict oft-repeated claims that such stops are necessary to get guns off the street."[5]

As of March 2022, Los Angeles Police Department officers are no longer able to use minor infractions as a pretext to investigate drivers, bikers, or pedestrians for more serious offenses unless they have sufficient evidence to support the incursion.[6] In the months after the policy went into place, pretextual stops for offenses such as an air freshener hanging in the rearview mirror or expired registrations dropped to 12 percent of stops, from 21 percent.[7] While I believe we need to go farther, this is a start for un-arresting the mobility of Black drivers.

Work is also being done to reform police enforcement against pedestrians and cyclists.

Pedestrian advocacy organizations such as Cal Walks, BikeWalk KC, and America Walks are working to repeal jaywalking laws in their communities and around the country. A few states have recognized that jaywalking laws do not have the intended effect of making streets safer and are not being enforced fairly or equitably, and they have repealed these laws. Virginia became the first state to do so in January 2021,[8] followed by California and Nevada and the cities of Kansas City, Missouri; Denver, Colorado; and most recently New York City in September 2024.[9,10]

Bicycle helmet laws have been repealed in some jurisdictions (although they are still supported by National Transportation Safety Board).[11] In 2022, the Board of Health of King County, Washington, which includes Seattle, voted 11–2 to repeal a helmet law after advocates presented data showing disparities in enforcement for people of color and unhoused people, as well as research showing it did not improve traffic safety.[12]

Another important step is for jurisdictions to reduce or eliminate court fines and fees associated with driving laws and pedestrian, bicycle, and e-scooter policies. The budgets of many municipalities rely heavily on fines and fees from driving violations, which provides a financial incentive to issue tickets for minor violations. Places with larger African American populations are more likely to rely heavily on these revenue sources.[13] These fines and fees can create severe financial hardship and arrest the mobility of residents, exacerbating the negative impacts of racial bias in policing.

RETHINK URBAN PLANNING AND POLICY

"Building empathy does not have to be a daunting task," writes Veronica O. Davis.[14] I believe that building empathy requires a culture shift. Racist urban planning practices in the past did not just take place at an agency level but were supported by a political system that made it possible to implement such policies.

"One thing we have to be clear about is whatever institution . . . is committing to racial equity—a DOT, Department of Housing, or Mayor's office—that institution must go through an internal transformation, because without the internal transformation, why should we have any confidence that an institution that has embedded racism has executed harms in our neighborhoods for many generations is now all of a sudden in a place to improve life outcomes for racially marginalized people?," said Equiticity's Olatunji Oboi Reed.[15]

We need to get to the root of how planning investments are made, how communities are designed, and the people who are involved. Culture change might be a long-term prospect, but it is doable. And we need to start with how we plan, design, and engineer our cities. And we need to rethink any plan or design that doesn't center the needs and concerns of Black people. As Reed says, "Why should racial equity pick and choose where it's going to be impactful? It must impact *everything*."

Plan for Change

Planners, designers, consultants, and agencies don't have to wait for policy reform to start making institutional and cultural change or change at the team or project level. This may be one of the most powerful ways to resist the dominant culture that is maintained by White societal norms and to create change.

Although planning institutions are becoming slightly more diverse, the culture, especially that of government agencies, is mired in an archaic system that doesn't consider issues of equity. It requires concerted effort to change that culture and embrace equity-driven approaches to planning.

In response to the murder of George Floyd in 2020, industries around the country brought in diversity, equity, and inclusion (DEI) professionals as part of their supposed effort to address institutional racism in the workplace. According to LinkedIn, the number of chief diversity and inclusion officer positions grew by 168.9 percent between 2019 and 2022, peaking in 2020–2021.[16] Along with these hires were commitments to increase diversity in the workforce. But this change was short-lived. Workforce analytics company Revelio Labs reported that layoffs in late 2022 greatly affected DEI professionals and the numbers of diverse hires.[17] DEI roles were eliminated from companies much faster than non-DEI roles; as of December 2022, the twelve-month attrition rate was 31 percent for DEI roles and 21 percent for non-DEI roles. There was also a significant decline in diverse hires during this same period.

The lack of prioritization of DEI within an organization becomes exceptionally clear when these positions become the first to go. DEI within an organization should be much more than a role; it should be integrated into the culture of an organization. Culture change doesn't happen overnight, so leadership within planning agencies should bring DEI into their work as a part of the long game.

One organization that has brought DEI into the culture of the institution is the Southern California Association of Governments (SCAG), the country's largest metropolitan planning organization. SCAG oversees the planning and policy initiatives for six counties (Imperial, Los Angeles, Orange, Riverside, San Bernardino, and Ventura), 191 cities, and 19 million residents. In this area of southern California, Black households have a median income that is more than $35,000 less than White households.[18] Similarly, Hispanic full-time workers are three times more likely to live in poverty than their White counterparts.[19]

Native Americans in the region have the least access to employment opportunities via all transportation modes, and Hispanic residents are most likely to live in high-risk areas for pedestrian- or bicyclist-involved collisions.[20,21] Black commuters experience the longest travel times on public transit, nearly fifty-six minutes, compared with other racial and ethnic groups.[22] These factors contribute to the chronic arrested mobility experienced by these communities.

In 2020, SCAG's Regional Council adopted Resolution 20-623-2, which asserts that systemic racism is a human rights and public health crisis.[23] The resolution called for the formation of an ad hoc Special Committee on Equity & Social Justice to define and implement SCAG's plan to advance racial equity.[24] I was brought in as a consultant to facilitate Special Committee meetings and advise on strategic ways to center equity in its overall goals.

In 2021, the committee released its final report with a racial equity action plan that called for the development of an equity vision and goals guide, policies and metrics, and resources through the Sustainable Communities Program to promote environmental justice. The plan recommended assessing and realigning policies, including equity assessments in staff reports, expanding racial equity trainings, exploring research partnerships, and partnering on capacity-building with community-based organizations and stakeholders.[25] "As a regional planning organization, understanding the disparities and inequities resulting from geography and the built environment is central to SCAG's work to plan for a more racially just, equitable future," states the report.[26]

The committee established four goals. The first is to shift the organizational culture to one focused on inclusion, diversity, equity, and awareness (IDEA). This involves establishing an IDEA team to update the action plan and integrate their work into SCAG's strategic plan.

The second is to center racial equity in SCAG's regional policy and planning. This includes mandatory equity trainings for board members and the preparation of quarterly racial equity indicator reports, increasing opportunity for participation in SCAG committees by people from the community, particularly community-based organizations, and developing equity goals and policies.

The third goal is to encourage racial equity in local planning conversations by providing information to elected officials and local planners (such as fact sheets and tools to promote racial equity), supporting data requests and creating tools for information sharing for anyone who requests them, providing resources to help local organizations work most effectively with community-based organizations and integrate them into the planning process, building planning capacity in lower-resourced jurisdictions, and refining equity goals and evaluation criteria for their Sustainable Communities Program. "We have a lot of member agencies within the 191 cities," says Kome Ajise, executive director of SCAG. "Some have more capacity than others and we wanted to be in a place where we can help." For example, he said, "The city of LA doesn't need our help because they're big enough. But then there are the cities of Bell Gardens and Carter, which are all small cities that don't have the same capacity." SCAG can make sure that the best practices are available to the cities that need them, said Ajise.

The fourth goal is to be active and amplify. This includes collaborating on public information campaigns, strengthening relationships with other municipal planning offices, exploring partnership opportunities with community-based organizations (CBOs), and developing an inclusive economic recovery strategy.[27]

Ajise reports that three years in, the goals have been so fully integrated into the day-to-day practices of the agency that they've scaled back on the required reporting. The regular reporting had its intended effect of creating a cultural shift where IDEA strategies are integrated into the day-to-day operations of each department.

"Now we're trying to upgrade what we call our CBO strategy," he says, to build off of what they've accomplished and where there are gaps. "It used to be, we just found them, brought them to the table. We're finding it's not that easy, because these are all volunteers and they need to be paid. So, if you really want that benefit to the fullest extent, then you need to put some budget to it."

Paying CBOs is easier said than done because the government bureaucracy has strict reporting and contracting guidelines. SCAG's current workaround is paying CBOs with grants from their Sustainable Communities Program.[28] However, these are short-term projects and they're limiting in that they tend to be one-offs. SCAG is working to find a better solution.

SCAG's work shows that with a concerted effort it doesn't have to take that long to change agency culture. With buy-in at all levels of SCAG, it only took a couple years for it to become second nature.

I showcase one example of a partnership from the Sustainable Communities Program grant that developed out of this work in Chapter 5.

Engage in Restorative Justice

In order for the field of planning to effectively reckon with its history of intentional harms done to Black people and communities, restorative justice must be considered. This means trying to actively repair the harm that has been inflicted on Black communities. The Restorative Council explains, "Restorative justice brings those harmed by crime or conflict and those responsible for the harm into communication, enabling everyone affected by a particular incident to play a part in repairing the harm and finding a positive way forward."[29] It's a model that involves accountability and repair.

Veronica Davis believes that "restoration" is critical. She writes. "It connects cultural anthropology, you might say, to present-day outreach and decision-making."[30]

Michael Kelley from BikeWalk KC says, "I sincerely hope that the efforts of our community to remove jaywalking [laws] is stopping the immediate harm." He continued, "But more importantly, I hope that it gets us to begin to ask the questions of how we can begin to do right by the communities that have been harmed for so long. . . . So restorative justice is not only stopping the harm, but also doing more to specifically target investments in a way that moves beyond just the blanket, 'We need to fix infrastructure everywhere,' and specifically goes to, 'How can we use infrastructure as a means of supporting the broader needs of a community?,' because justice is not just about doing what is right and wrong, in my view. I think it really is about how do you make someone whole? And that can't come from just stopping a harm. It has to come from going beyond that to support more of the needs of what a community really is asking for."[31]

That is where we can bring in strategies such as *targeted universalism*. Targeted universalism, developed by john a. powell of UC Berkeley's Othering & Belonging Institute, advocates for prioritizing the problems experienced by the most marginalized people, to the benefit of the rest of society.[32] It's a policy solution that focuses on race in program and investment priorities. We can use targeted universalism as a means for restorative justice in city and community planning. As a tool for un-arresting mobility, it's a matter of working with and connecting with Black communities and Black-led organizations to identify where community members don't feel safe, what are their challenges with getting around, and what makes it difficult for them to feel comfortable in a community.

Black communities that were harmed by policies and practices such as redlining and urban renewal should receive restitution. In the world of planning this could look like investing money or providing monetary benefits to restoring land or property to the original owners. In 2022, the US Department of Transportation introduced the Reconnecting Communities Pilot Program, "a first-of-its-kind initiative to reconnect communities that are cut off from opportunity and burdened by past transportation infrastructure decisions."[33] The program has a number of limitations—one being that the $1 billion distributed over five years is nowhere near the amount of funding necessary—but it's an acknowledgment of the harms done and a step toward active repair.[34] Hopefully this initial funding will be the beginning of full investment to restore these communities that have been harmed by government actions.

As of August 2024, forty-two communities have received grants from the Reconnecting Communities program. One of those grants went to the City of Syracuse, New York, where removal of the Interstate 81 viaduct began in 2022. When it was built in the 1950s, the highway tore apart the working-class Black neighborhood of the 15th ward.[35,36]

With funding and support from the US Department of Housing and Urban Development, I'm providing technical assistance on the community engagement part of that project to help ensure that the outcome isn't just a torn-down highway but is a true restoration as defined by the community. My role is to facilitate the City of Syracuse's efforts to rebuild trust with residents through restorative justice. This involves ensuring that the historically displaced communities, particularly those affected by the original construction of Interstate 81, are central to the planning and decision-making processes around current and future projects. By elevating resident voices, restoring accountability, and fostering transparency in both housing redevelopment and transportation projects, the aim is to repair the harm caused by past injustices, rebuild community connections, and ensure that these initiatives lead to equitable outcomes for all residents. The plan will focus on community and economic development goals by promoting revitalization efforts through street-level retail, community spaces, and urban place-making.[37]

Another restorative justice project funded through the Reconnecting Communities program is the restoration of the historically Black Rondo neighborhood in Saint Paul, Minnesota. In Rondo, over 700 homes and 300 businesses were lost when Interstate 94 was constructed. To begin the restoration process, ReConnect Rondo will use $2 million in funds to construct a community land bridge over I-94.[38,39] The $2 million falls short of the $6 million needed to realize the full project, but hopefully more investment will follow to close the $4 million gap. It's hard to say whether the project will be completed if the funding doesn't come through from the federal government. But if local agencies and leaders participate in advocacy, there's a chance for at least portions of the project to be carried out through local, regional, and state funding mechanisms.

The idea of the land bridge came out of a community study conducted by the Urban Land Institute that found that physical reconnection was important to restoring and reconnecting a community torn apart by urban renewal transportation investments and would contribute to livability of the neighborhood. The bridge would be more than a means to cross over I-94 on foot; it would include a vibrant design and would support mixed-use development and green space. The district would prioritize Black-owned business development, providing an opportunity for African American leadership and ownership.[40]

It's exciting to see the momentum toward restorative justice in planning, and I hope these efforts will lead to more funding from federal and state departments of transportation for community-based efforts that can pave the way for reconnecting and restoring Black communities.

Prioritize Mobility Investments in Black Communities

Transit infrastructure has been a boon to many cities around the United States, helping reduce greenhouse gas emissions and unclog city streets. However, transit investments have largely advantaged White, educated, and higher-income people,[41] and where investments were made in lower-income neighborhoods, those communities often experienced high housing prices and displacement due to gentrification.[42] This happens when policymakers and planners don't put up guardrails that help to maintain affordable housing and ensure that historic residents can stay in their communities.

Lower-income Black communities should be prioritized for multimodal mobility investments with safeguards to protect residents from displacement. Portland's BIKETOWN system, mentioned in the Introduction, is a great example of how this is being done. Not only are docking stations more prominent in lower-income neighborhoods, but the BIKETOWN for All program helps community members use the system. Additionally, in 2020, Metro, the regional governing agency of the Portland Metro region that covers three counties, introduced a ballot measure to fund transportation projects in some of the most dangerous traffic corridors, which happened to be the communities with the highest concentrations of people of color.[43]

The measure didn't pass, but the groundwork was laid for other ways to fund the investments.[44] For example, the high-fatality network along the 82nd Avenue corridor in East Portland, one of the most diverse communities in the area, is being funded jointly by Metro and the City of Portland.[45] Improvements began in 2023 and are expected to be completed by 2027.

In the next chapter we'll look at the work of Equiticity to bring a Go Hub to the North Lawndale community in Chicago.

Improve the Relationship of Black Communities with Mobility

Olatunji Oboi Reed believes that more needs to be done to help Black community members develop a better relationship with mobility. As suggested in the Alejandro Jodorowsky quote, "Birds born in a cage think flying is an illness," Black Americans' relationship with mobility won't be magically healed once investments are made.

Reed said to me that he believes that a solution to this is "funding the socialization that happens through community mobility rituals" (CMRs). These include community bicycle rides, neighborhood walking tours, public transit excursions, group scooter rides, and open street festivals. He believes that "it's the socialization we need around mobility, helping people reimagine their connection, their relationship to our neighborhoods and to modes of travel and to mobility."

When he first got into biking, Reed would put his bike in his trunk, drive to Chicago's lakefront trail, and bike there. He was afraid to ride on the streets of Chicago until he participated in a Critical Mass Ride. Critical Mass is a movement that started in the 1990s that organized hundreds of people to take over the streets in their communities with whatever wheel-based nonmotorized vehicle they had in order to protest infrastructure that served mostly cars.[46] Although Critical Mass rides have mostly fizzled out in Chicago, they have been replaced with smaller, independently organized rides that Equiticity organizes.

Reed points to Ciclovía Recreativa in Bogotá, Colombia, a program that, each Sunday, closes down miles of roadway to vehicle traffic and opens the space to bicycles and pedestrian traffic only. It's essentially a big party every Sunday, with booths, dance parties, and community along the streets. The program has spread across Latin America to places such as Santiago de Cali, Colombia; Mexico City; and Santiago, Chile.[47] It has spread to the

United States with programs including New York City's Summer Streets, Los Angeles's CicLAvia, and Portland, Oregon's Summer Parkways. Ciclovía is an excellent example of active transportation-oriented rituals and celebrations that create social cohesion. A team of researchers from around the Americas found in a 2020 study of Ciclovía in Bogotá and Santiago de Cali that people became even more connected to others in their community through these events. So not only did it increase the level of physical activity community members participated in, it also provided interaction between different socioeconomic groups and promoted social cohesion and social capital.[48] The event also resulted in a reduction in perceptions of crime and an increase in how safe people felt.

Reed's organization, Equiticity, coordinated with the Harris Community Action Team to look into implementing an open streets program in Chicago similar to Ciclovía.[49] Although an integrated, miles-long event such as those in Latin America hasn't been realized in Chicago as of yet, Equiticity is taking smaller steps to produce the same results through CMRs.

Equiticity hosts five types of CMRs: community bicycle rides, neighborhood walking tours, public transit excursions, group scooter rolls, and open street festivals. He notes that seven elements are essential to these rituals.

The first is a ritualistic schedule. This can be as frequent or infrequent as necessary, once a month, once a week, always on the same day. "The rhythmic schedule is critical because when that schedule is rhythmic and it's easy to understand, people are more likely to fit their lifestyle around the schedule," Reed told me.

The second is having a hyperlocal focus. "The audience we're prioritizing for Equiticity, given the racial equity movement, are Black and Brown people who live in the neighborhood where the CMR is taking place," he says. "It doesn't mean we're excluding people, anyone's welcome to come, however the audience we're the most concerned with participating are Black and Brown people who live in the neighborhood." He notes that when these two things come together, rhythmic schedule and hyperlocal focus, there's a long-term sense of community being built. Riders will come back week after week when they know someone who will be there and will feel more like they're part of something larger.

The third element is shared customs. Equiticity does a call and response during their rides, which helps form a bond between riders and also announces that the group is there. "It's a way to take over spaces to send a message to us and others that this is our neighborhood, that this is our street, this is our park, and we're not going to allow other people's perspectives to shape how we practice ownership of our space," says Reed.

The fourth element is prioritizing socialization over physical activity. By having it be a social event, you're showing it's not a race, it's not a competition, that this is something the group is doing together.

The fifth is focusing on racialized healing by creating an integrated space to help heal the historical barriers of race. Creating this space in a fun, open environment could lead to deeper healing in the community.

The sixth is reducing barriers to participation. Make sure that the process to participate is easy to understand, and create an atmosphere where everyone feels welcome.

CMRs actively disrupt the status quo by reclaiming the streets that were designed for cars and by joyfully taking over communities that have been overlooked.

CMRs have ripple effects around the communities. The presence of these lively, fun, engaging, and community-oriented events shows the vibrancy of the communities, which can attract more retail and encourage more investments and discourage violence.

Conduct Deep Community Engagement

To effectively invest in mobility in Black communities, federal, state, regional, and local governments must fund and administer planning processes that involve deep equitable and inclusive community engagement. That means going beyond the requisite "community meeting" held at a downtown office in the middle of a workday. Deep community engagement involves affected community members in every single stage of the planning process. Community members know what they need for mobility much more than an engineer or planner from the city, regional, or state transportation department. In fact, all professionals know that the "real" experts are community members. Defining and designing a solution without their perspective, their ideas, their buy-in, and their support doesn't solve anything. This requires heightened levels of self-awareness and humility, recognizing that planning professionals may not have all the answers.

The US Department of Transportation has created a guide on meaningful public involvement that acknowledges the need to go beyond the one-way meetings that have become the norm when checking the box of "community engagement."[50] However, it takes practice for planners, engineers, and other transportation professionals to work deeply and consistently with the community on an ongoing basis.

Lynn Peterson, author of *Roadways for People: Rethinking Transportation Planning and Engineering*, suggests a community solutions-based approach for advancing change at a project level.[51] This requires including community voices in meaningful ways at every stage of the process, from problem statement to implementing the project. The community members should see all of the plans, weigh in, and help define the solutions. This must be done through deep engagement and connection with community-based organizations that serve the community.

Peterson writes from the perspective of a privileged White woman who realized that she had been complicit in planning decisions that arrest mobility. She realized that one planner, or even a team of planners and engineers, especially if they are White, cannot un-arrest the mobility of Black Americans alone. It needs to be a community-engaged, collaborative approach.

There are a variety of tools for involving communities in the planning process that are rooted in racial equity approaches.[52] Community-based participatory research is a community-centric form of research, and asset-based community development is a method of working with community to enact community development by starting with who is already contributing to community efforts. Both approaches are useful in understanding how to approach community engagement.[53–55]

Design Transportation Solutions Beyond Enforcement

Unequal enforcement of driving, biking, pedestrian, and scooting laws isn't just a police or law enforcement issue; this is also an issue for planners and engineers. They are tasked with designing our communities and transportation infrastructure. If we're assuming that speed limits are the way to manage safe driving practices, we're viewing planning solutions through a myopic lens. Planners and engineers can design mobility solutions through a racial justice framework so that safety efforts do not come at the expense of Black community members.

For example, speed can be managed effectively through design instead of by speed limits alone (which would involve enforcement). Beautifying the medians and adding speed bumps do more to limit speed than lowering a posted speed limit.

Veronica Davis describes the work she did in Washington, DC, in 2015, one of the first cities in the country to embrace Vision Zero. She notes that it was an example of both the possibilities and shortcomings of such a model. The possibilities came in the form of community outreach. Of all the cities that had adopted Vision Zero, Washington, DC, was the first to do meaningful outreach as a part of the development process.

"Over the course of a summer, we had ten meetings on street corners around the city, a youth summit with over two hundred young people, two meetings with special advocacy groups, and meetings with over thirty-five city agencies," she writes. "We did not just inform people; we also engaged with them and used their feedback and stories to shape the plan. As an example, after talking with a group of young Black teens at the youth summit, we removed all enforcement related to people walking and biking."[56]

Davis lauds DC's equity approach. But she also saw some shortcomings to the plan. "DC's Vision Zero plan correctly focused on behaviors that lead to deaths and fatalities," she writes. "However, the plan should have recommended a comprehensive evaluation of *all* the transportation laws and the removal of any that were not supported by data or did not lead to safer streets."[57] And in this process, there would also be a role of planners to think about solutions through the lens of street design rather than purely through enforcement.

Jersey City, New Jersey, has found a way to approach planning solutions beyond enforcement that doesn't require large, expensive projects: *tactical urbanism*, which consists of low-cost, scalable design projects such as pedestrian plazas, parklets, and pop-up bike lanes.[58] Jersey City was able to reach zero deaths on city streets in 2022 with the help of this approach.[59] Barkha Patel, also a former Rutgers graduate student of mine, is director of the new Department of Infrastructure, and her team worked with a planning firm, Street Plans, to achieve that goal.[60] The city reconfigured intersections with traffic paint, delineators, thermoplastic striping, and increasing visibility at crosswalks in over eighty-five intersections.

"These kinds of pilots have become the city's preferred method of engagement," wrote John Surico in a *Bloomberg CityLab* story about Jersey City's successes. "Community meetings in advance of road redesigns famously tend to go sideways while the actual physicality of a demonstration helps to build consensus, albeit imperfect. It also reaches people who might not be able to make it to a meeting or Zoom at 6 p.m. on a weeknight. Instead, it meets them where they live."[61]

This method is especially useful in an incredibly diverse city with over 27 percent of residents being Hispanic, over 25 percent Asian, 23 percent White, and 20 percent Black.[62] Tactical urbanism meets community members where they're at through temporary design that they can experience themselves and help planners make adjustments in real time before any permanent changes are made.

Another example of making streets safer through design is the *complete streets* approach. Queens Boulevard in New York City, previously known as the "Boulevard of Death," received a federal grant of $23.75 million to redesign the corridor in December 2023.[63] Efforts will focus on expanding and reconstructing road medians by putting in a raised pedestrian mall and bike path, reconfiguring slip ramps, improving accessibility at bus stops, and adding new landscaping, lighting, and public seating. These efforts create a more livable place for everyone while helping to slow traffic down in an organic way.

Engage with Biking and the Micromobility Industry on Solutions

As planners, engineers, and policymakers, we often take on the burden of creating safe communities all on our own. And that's true in a lot of ways because it is ultimately our responsibility to keep citizens safe. But there's also a responsibility on behalf of manufacturers to make their equipment safe and ensure that it meets legal requirements.

For example, when you're sold a bike in a city where a certain type of light is required at night, you then have to purchase the light separately. The cyclist who purchased the bike might not even know or think of getting a light unless a person at the store mentions that it's the law or that it would be a good idea. The onus of complying with the law is completely on the bike owner. Contrast this to purchasing a car. A car won't be sold without proper lighting that would then comply with the law. A car buyer would never have to think about whether to purchase additional equipment in order to comply with the law. Manufacturers should sell their micromobility devices with the various local laws in mind.

This is related to arrested mobility because if a person uses this equipment without a safety feature required by the local law, it increases their risk of coming into contact with law enforcement. That is a matter of safety for Black people because every interaction with the police has the potential to be deadly.

Therefore, there's an opportunity to work with the industry to make changes that could embed safety features into equipment.

Bike safety organizations and bike advocacy groups are already keyed into local laws in almost every major city. There is an opportunity to work with these groups to compel the industry to build their micromobility vehicles with the necessary equipment to meet local laws and reduce the potential for police interactions.

These recommendations show that planners and engineers can play a big part in un-arresting mobility for Black Americans by changing the way we do our work.

REMOVE POLICING FROM MOBILITY ENFORCEMENT

The current system of enforcement makes streets less safe for Black and Brown Americans, putting them at risk of arrest for what may be a minor infraction. Should the police be involved in mobility enforcement at all?

Equiticity's Reed believes that they should not. He believes that Chicago's police force in particular is "a rogue institution that won't even take direction from the mayor," he said. "They won't even hold to a court and enforce consent decree. This is a rogue institution that has no business trying to improve traffic safety in our neighborhoods. And every time there is a role for them, it comes with harms and risk in our neighborhoods."[64]

Most cities that are making some changes in traffic policing are taking a piecemeal approach.

In 2021 Philadelphia became the first major city in the United States to ban some low-level traffic stops such as a damaged bumper, broken tail light, or unfastened registration plates.[65,66] These were considered "targeted" traffic stops. After the ban went into effect in March 2022, the city saw a 54 percent drop in specific types of these targeted low-level violations. But the proportion of traffic stops of Black drivers remained the same, which is a failure of the policy.[67]

Pittsburgh enacted a ban on low-level traffic stops around the same time with similar results: Stops have decreased, but disparities in policing still exist.[68] However, like any new law, it takes some time to see long-term changes.

The lack of systemic change from these one-off policy changes is why Jordan Blair Woods, legal scholar and law professor at University of Arizona, believes there needs to be a wholesale reframing of who enforces traffic. "Piecemeal constitutional and statutory interventions that attempt to limit aspects of police authority during traffic stops are insufficient to address systemic racial and economic injustices in traffic policing," wrote Woods in 2021, in the most thorough framework for civilian traffic enforcement.[69] "Rather, these problems necessitate structural police reform and require a fundamental rethinking of the role of police in the traffic space."[70]

In Los Angeles, tamika l. butler and my team at Equitable Cities facilitated focus groups in partnership with the LA Department of Transportation (LADOT) in 2023 to help identify how the city could find ways to move away from traffic enforcement by the police.

"We heard from community members that they wanted a holistic approach to understanding traffic violence in a way that accounts for the stress that community members experience related to racial discrimination and the fear that many of us have as it relates to being stopped by police," butler wrote in an email to me. One solution would be to move from a punitive approach to preventive.

"Prevention means that government should invest in things like infrastructure and social programs. When you look at the infrastructure in low-income communities of color, there have been years of intentional neglect that should be corrected rather than relying on enforcement. Focus on street design can increase traffic safety without increasing police budgets." What they were asking for was to see transportation safety much more broadly. "There was hope," butler says, "that there would be more broad and authentic community engagement to ensure that people's mobility was centered and improving traffic safety outcomes, not just the speed of cars."

LADOT is moving forward on recommendations we provided to reduce armed traffic enforcement, including incorporating definitions and research on self-enforcing infrastructure (e.g., using street designs to compel slowing down rather than increasing surveillance) into current projects and programs and prioritizing this method in low-income communities and communities of color; evaluating whether enforcing moving violations improves traffic safety without undue impact on low-income people and communities of color; and investigating requirements in order to create an unarmed, care-based team to respond to traffic calls.[71]

Jordan Blair Woods recommends shifting funding from police to non-police entities, which LADOT is working toward.

Some communities are going further to remove police from all traffic enforcement, including Berkeley, California; Lansing, Michigan; Ramsey County, Minnesota; and Virginia.[72]

The City of Berkeley, California, is looking at replacing mobility enforcement by police with civilian traffic enforcement.[73] The proposal was developed from listening sessions with the community. The Berkeley Department of Transportation (BerkDOT), in collaboration with Fehr & Peers and my company, Equitable Cities, conducted a series of community listening sessions in October and November 2021 with diverse groups of high school students, college students, and religious minority groups of color in Berkeley. The primary objectives were to explore the experiences and perceptions of racial justice and transportation safety and to identify potential actions to improve mobility justice for racial minorities.

We heard about negative experiences around safety on the Bay Area Rapid Transit and Alameda–Contra Costa Transit systems, including discrimination and harassment from other riders and actions by law enforcement. Participants in all groups expressed apprehension about being treated unfairly or harmed by police officers because of their race, age, or religion. The college students and religious minority groups supported reallocating traffic enforcement responsibilities away from the police to unarmed city employees, which could reduce the disproportionate burden and fear placed on communities of color.

When the idea of removing police officers from traffic and mobility enforcement was presented to a female college student participant, she said, "I think that it would be a good idea because we've seen time and time again that police officers are likely to kill people of color especially black people for no reason just because of a traffic violation."

"[When they see] you're an African American you're screwed," said another female high school student participant.

Many participants placed their experiences of discrimination from law enforcement within the context of police shootings of other Black Americans. "I think about many stories over the past couple of years about how the police have killed or hurt black men and other people of color," a female religious minority participant said.

"If the city or if local government cares about people of color and marginalized communities, they're going to take steps towards making sure that never happens again," said a female college student participant.

The findings from the Berkeley Department of Transportation community listening sessions reveal the multifaceted nature of mobility challenges faced by communities of color in Berkeley. They underscore the urgent need for targeted interventions and policy changes to ensure equitable mobility and access to opportunities for all residents, particularly those from marginalized communities.

While it's still unclear how Berkeley plans to carry out the civilian enforcement of traffic laws, James Blair Woods laid out a framework that would involve changes in three key areas:

- Reevaluating traffic codes that currently enable police discretion in traffic stops. The first aspect of this is trimming state and local traffic laws and circumstances to "include only traffic violations that put motorists or pedestrians at risk of imminent danger."[74] These may include driving a stolen vehicle, hit-and-run, or vehicle racing.[75]
- Establishing traffic agencies that are completely separate from police departments. These agencies would hire their own traffic monitors that are not law enforcement officials. In-person traffic stops and some enforcement might happen through automation.[76]
- Reducing or removing the financial and professional incentive that often drives biased enforcement (e.g., the traffic fines and fees system and traffic ticket quotas linked to professional performance).[77]

Removing police from all traffic enforcement where no driver or pedestrian is in imminent danger effectively decriminalizes traffic violations. This is the kind of restructuring and rebuilding of a system that can happen when we look beyond the need for police. We've become so accustomed to the system that it can be difficult to see how it can be different.

Civilian response teams have been used successfully in other areas such as mental health calls to help reduce the number of police killings of people in a mental health crisis. According to a 2015 Treatment Advocacy Center report, people experiencing a mental health crisis are sixteen times more likely to be killed by police.[78] In Orland Park, Illinois, a Department of Justice grant helped scale up a Mobile Crisis Response Unit to divert mental health calls to co-response teams between mental health service organization Trinity Services and the local police, where the on-call mental health worker takes the lead on the response.[79] In Eugene, Oregon, Crisis Assistance Helping Out on the Streets (CAHOOTS) is an all-civilian mental health response unit that is staffed by the mental health service organization White Bird Clinic, funded by the City of Eugene through police funding since 1989; it was expanded to twenty-four-hour service with additional city funding in 2016.[80] The program has been a huge success: Of about 24,000 calls to CAHOOTS in 2019, only 311 required police backup.[81]

New technology such as surveillance devices becomes much less dangerous when it is not directly connected to police departments (see Chapter 3). If that direct line is removed, users have more barriers to contact, what social psychologist Jennifer Eberhardt calls "decision points of contact," and may make a decision other than calling the police.[82] It doesn't put a hard-and-fast barrier in place because White citizens are much more empowered to call the police, but it makes it less easy to do so.

Other reform efforts include requiring police training in nonviolent alternatives to deadly force and in conflict deescalation, requiring that police officers live in the communities where they work, and improving relations between Black communities and the police.

We need to rethink how police are used to enforce safety in society. It is clear that giving police more power does not make Black Americans safer. Yet the system of policing has been so conflated with safety that it takes a paradigm shift to see beyond it.

EMPOWER AND FOLLOW BLACK LEADERSHIP

It is imperative to center and empower Black leadership in planning and police restructuring efforts. In many cities, even in majority Black cities, biking, pedestrian, and micromobility advocacy groups are predominantly White-led. Although these groups have done a lot to advance advocacy for building protected bike lanes and pushing cities and states to invest in multimodal transportation, people from White-led organizations don't experience the daily mobility challenges of a Black person.

When I asked Olatunji Oboi Reed about the role advocacy groups can play in making change, he said, "Number one, they need to get out of the way—the leadership from a racial equity perspective, from a mobility justice perspective must come from Black and Brown people."

White-led organizations and advocacy groups can use their privilege, their funding, and their connections to help advocate for mobility justice initiatives put forward by Black-led organizations. For example, the organization New Urban Mobility Alliance, which is a non–Black-led organization, has supported my company, Equitable Cities, by providing funding for the arrested mobility report we published in March 2023.[83,84] A lot of times allyship is just this, seeing where important work is being done by Black-led organizations, following their lead, and supporting them in whatever way they want or need it. This can also be achieved at a more systemic level when agencies, such as SCAG, commit to building the capacity of Black-led organizations to partner with or contract with government entities to carry out DEI programs in mobility.

The solutions in this chapter addresses policy, planning, and advocacy. Planners, policymakers, and advocates can use these to push for change to help un-arrest mobility and move toward mobility justice.

FIVE

Arrested Mobility Solutions in Action

"It's up to all of us—Black, white, everyone—no matter how well-meaning we think we might be, to do the honest, uncomfortable work of rooting [racism] out."

—Michelle Obama

Countless people are working to un-arrest mobility around the United States and the world. In this chapter I showcase people from around the United States who are championing community engagement in the planning process, community-led programming, individual advocacy, and legal challenges to arrested mobility.

COMMUNITY MOBILITY EMPOWERMENT IN NORTH LAWNDALE, CHICAGO

For decades, the predominantly Black community of North Lawndale in West Chicago has largely been neglected by the city.

In "The Case for Reparations" in *The Atlantic*, Ta-Nehisi Coates tells the story of North Lawndale resident Clyde Ross.[1] After growing up in Mississippi and then serving in the Army during World War II, in 1947 Ross moved to Chicago. He was one of 6 million Black Americans who moved north to escape the segregation and violence of the South during the Great Migration.[2] What Ross found was a different form of segregation.

In 1961, Ross and his wife purchased a home in North Lawndale. The neighborhood was transitioning from a majority Jewish into a middle-class Black community. Buying in North Lawndale gave the Rosses access to the American Dream, but they couldn't secure a traditional mortgage because North Lawndale was redlined and deemed "too risky."[3] Instead, the Rosses purchased the home "on contract," which is "a predatory agreement that combined all the responsibilities of homeownership with all the disadvantages of renting—while offering the benefits of neither," writes Coates. They weren't the only ones who were in this situation on their block. Predatory lenders used redlined communities such as North Lawndale to take advantage of Black people. Redlining and predatory lending began a new era of extortion and disinvestment of Black communities.

People like Clyde Ross recognized the racist housing practices and fought back. In fact, the neighborhood became a base for the Civil Rights movement in the North. In 1966, Dr. Martin Luther King Jr. moved to North Lawndale to protest the slum conditions and unfair and racist housing policies.[4] When King was murdered in 1968, North Lawndale became the center of destruction rooted in the decades of anger from systemic and overt racism. "Bulldozers cleared away the charred debris, and West Side residents—most of whom were blameless in the violence—hoped their communities would be rebuilt," reads a 2018 *Chicago Tribune* story of the events. "But after five decades, why are pockets of the West Side still decimated?"[5]

The experts in the *Chicago Tribune* story see the riots as the main reason the neighborhood was "destroyed." However, it is clear that many earlier urban planning practices contributed to its disinvestment. Lifelong North Lawndale resident Rochelle Jackson believes that the community is far from destroyed. But Jackson and others have been asking why the city hasn't invested in North Lawndale and other historically Black communities.

The answer, of course is that institutional and systemic racism result in the prioritization of investments in White neighborhoods. Disinvestment in Black and Brown neighborhoods is still visible in neighborhoods that had been redlined.

In 2022, the office of the Cook County treasurer, Maria Pappas, released a study "Maps of Inequality: From Redlining to Urban Decay and the Black Exodus."[6] The study points to a single redlined block in North Lawndale where, between 1938 and 1973, one in four properties were vacant, but now that has increased to nearly two in four.

Fortunately, community advocates such as Rochelle Jackson and groups such as Equiticity have focused on un-arresting mobility in North Lawndale. Equiticity and their executive director, Olatunji Oboi Reed (referenced throughout this book), focus on creating mobility programs and transforming legislation and policy through a racial equity framework. Rochelle Jackson serves on the community advisory council and works with several other community members to ensure that Equiticity hears directly from community members.

One of the major projects they've been working on over the past several years is The Go Hub, a Black-centered mobility initiative.

The Go Hub Vision

Some programs that will be part of The Go Hub are in progress, such as the Community Mobility Rituals mentioned in Chapter 4. To realize the full vision, Equiticity is raising funds to buy the building in which The Go Hub will be housed, across the street from the Pulaski "L" rail station on the Pink Line. The project is designed to restore the neighborhood's vitality by way of mobility.

The transit-friendly, walkable location is essential to the success of The Go Hub. "One of the transformative outcomes is the financial burden being lifted from a family when they don't have the expense of a car," says Reed. "You know, they're in walking distance to go home, and they can borrow an electric vehicle when they need it, or they can borrow a bike when they need it for school. . . . They have the devices there to use at their discretion."

The Go Hub will offer multiple forms of transportation to members: bicycles, e-bikes, e-scooters, and electric cars. The membership model is a way to build trust, not only between the members and the organization but among the community members.

In typical membership models, the trust is usually more one-way, where the lender needs some kind of assurance that the borrower will return the device. That is usually established through collateral in the form of your credit card. But that's a barrier for a lot of people in a place like North Lawndale. So the trust is in buying into the community aspect of the model. Members have shared responsibility and shared experiences in mobility. Membership rates will be affordable and will offer unlimited access to services within The Go Hub and benefits such as reduced prices for e-bike, e-scooter, and car sharing services run by third-party companies.

The Go Hub will offer classes on bike maintenance and safety. Staff members will be on site to help troubleshoot or answer questions.

Reed is hoping to have retail on site, such as a coffee shop or a bookstore, elements that help create an atmosphere of community. Creating a multipurpose space invites people to stay in the space rather than just pass through it.

Other plans for the space include a semipermanent art exhibit that showcases the history of the neighborhood, especially Martin Luther King Jr. and the Civil Rights movement. Art by contemporary Black artists will be displayed in the indoor and outdoor spaces.

The outdoor space will be vibrant and inviting, with a calming garden and a stage to host concerts and live events by and for the community.

"It's only recently that people, organizations, government agencies have started to think about mobility hubs targeting a marginalized community, and what does that look like when their audience is Black, Brown, or Indigenous," says Reed. "And I don't know of many mobility hubs, both in the U.S. and around the world that combine what we would call 'software,' so that's like the word to socialize people, such as community mobility rituals."

What Reed means by "software" is the additional services that can help create a comfortable, welcoming environment for someone who is new to these vehicles and to support people who have been traumatized through a lifetime of systemic racism. Examples include providing training on how to use devices, staff on hand to help people troubleshoot or to answer questions about devices, and even therapeutic services such as a counseling center and wellness activities such as yoga and meditation specifically for the members of The Go Hub. This software complements the "hardware" such as the building, the vehicles, and the devices (Figure 5-1).

FIGURE 5-1 This rendering of The Go Hub is not site specific but gives a sense of what it could look like from the exterior. There will be a spacious and green garden space for events and connecting with other members on the outside, and inside will be a community meeting place. (Rendering courtesy of Equiticity and created by Odile Compagnon)

The community built through The Go Hub can also be seen as software. The software is the connections with one another, the gathering in the public space or meeting up over a cup of coffee at an on-site coffee shop.

The Process of Getting There

The Go Hub has been designed by and for the community.

In 2021 Equiticity partnered with researchers at the University of Illinois and the Metropolitan Planning Council to look at how transportation affects access to jobs in predominantly Black neighborhoods on the South and West sides of Chicago.[7] Nearly three quarters of participants in the study "indicated that transportation was a barrier to getting and keeping a job." The report states, "Respondents often talked about the overall transportation experience as a burden and a source of stress."[8] Many residents feel safest traveling by car. If transit is too far from one's home to feel safe, a person who can afford a car is more likely to drive.

This community input served as the foundation of The Go Hub concept. The community engagement process was guided by a community advisory council made up of local stakeholders and individuals such as Rochelle Jackson, long-time transportation advocate and transportation and infrastructure chair of the North Lawndale Community Coordinating Council[9]; Derek Brown, founder of Boxing Out Negativity (a violence prevention program for youth)[10]; representatives from All Eyez On Me (an organization that delivers urgent needs to community members in the form of disaster assistance, youth development, and violence prevention); Firehouse Community Arts Center of Chicago; North Lawndale Employment Network; and YMEN, a leadership program for young men.

Importantly, these community partners were paid for their time serving on the council. Compensating partners "is really the key piece," says Remel Terry, Equiticity's director of programs in an interview. "We weren't just asking people to help support without figuring out how we help fund their support . . . leveraging the relationships that they had, pushing out the things that we were doing, so they had their own constituency base that they serve."

The focus groups referenced earlier were conducted in the community through the Equiticity partnership with researchers from the University of Illinois.[11] "One of the findings we uncovered in the research is the significant level of Black and Brown people's concerns around violence to the extent that it shapes our mode choice," says Reed. That's why many residents rely on cars to keep themselves safe. It's one of the major reasons Equiticity's work does not shun the use of vehicles. This doesn't mean that people don't use or need public transportation, but it needs to be reliable and safe. People need to be supported to feel comfortable using other forms of transportation. That is part of the goal of The Go Hub: to help people feel more comfortable with other modes of transportation.

The draft designs for The Go Hub, based on this research and input, were presented to 300 community members in a charrette. Participants formed small groups to talk about ideas and provide feedback.

This meeting was instrumental in giving community members a voice in the process. "When engineers and designers come into our neighborhood, they already have an idea of how they want our neighborhood to look," says Jackson in an interview. "So, we've had a lot of fights with the city government agencies and the people that they bring in as design engineers." The Go Hub development process, she emphasizes, was completely different; the engaged community process created a sense of ownership. "It's something *of* the community, not just *in* the community," says Terry.

One concern that The Go Hub needed to address was the threat of a gentrification. Transportation projects placed in predominantly Black and Brown neighborhoods have notoriously had the effect of raising prices and pushing historic residents out because of the increased investment.

Reed says that is something he is working to address at a scale beyond this project. Equiticity has been working with lawmakers and city planning departments to ensure that antidisplacement measures are put in place for all community improvement projects. The Chicago City Council has already passed ordinances to preserve a certain amount of affordable housing in quickly gentrifying neighborhoods in West and North Chicago.[12] In July 2024 an ordinance was proposed to preserve affordable housing in predominantly Latino neighborhoods of northwest Chicago, but no decision has been made as of yet.[13] Reed worries that because gentrification can happen quickly, and if ordinances are put into place after momentum has already taken hold, it could be too late for a number of residents. Because Equiticity isn't part of a city agency, they don't have the authority to make these changes, but they're still pushing.

What Equiticity does have control of is who The Go Hub serves. Membership is limited to low- or moderate-income people from the neighborhood. The ideas is that the mobility center will always be by and for the community, it will always be affordable to access, and it will always be a place of refuge in a world that is constantly at odds with their existence.

The Go Hub addresses arrested mobility by fostering safe, inclusive, and equitable transportation opportunities for Black and Brown residents. It will be more than just a mobility center; it is a community-driven initiative that integrates cultural, historical, and social elements into transportation planning.

This is a model for enhancing physical mobility while strengthening community bonds, promoting public health, and reducing environmental impacts. By addressing the root causes of mobility inequities—such as inadequate infrastructure and social exclusion—The Go Hub demonstrates how targeted, culturally informed interventions can dismantle the structures of arrested mobility.

Equiticity wants to expand The Go Hub to other neighborhoods in Chicago and to other cities around the country. North Lawndale is merely where this Go Hub movement begins.

LEARNING ABOUT RACIAL DISPARITIES IN LEVEE ACCESS IN RURAL LOUISIANA

The main street of the small town of St. Joseph, in northeastern Louisiana—called St. Joe by locals—extends up to the levee between the town and the Mississippi River. The levee, designed for flood protection, extends along approximately 1,607 miles of the Mississippi River.[14] As with many levees, the large mound of compacted clay and soil provides green space running along the top. In many places along the river the levee has publicly accessible trails that can be used for recreation. A proposed 130-mile bike and pedestrian trail along the levee could be a community resource and also bring in tourism to this isolated town.[15] But it is important that all community members feel welcome in the space.

In this majority Black community, the difference in who feels welcome or who can access the space depends quite a bit on race. Jamila Freightman, the Centers for Disease Control and Prevention Healthy Communities Manager at the Louisiana State University Agricultural Center (LSU AgCenter) and her team wanted to find out more about how Black and White community members felt about access to the levee for transportation or recreation.

In 2021 the LSU AgCenter team, in collaboration with the Louisiana Delta Trails Committee, brought me in to help conduct the focus groups for Black residents in St. Joseph and another town in the nearby East Carroll Parish, Lake Providence.

Before getting to the results of the focus groups, it is important to have some understanding of the demographics, the health outcomes, and the history of this part of Louisiana.

St. Joseph and Lake Providence, Louisiana

St. Joseph is a quaint community surrounded by live oak trees, with a charming main street that has seen more prosperous times. It is on the banks of the Mississippi River, and when paddlewheel ferries were replaced by railroads and highways as the primary means of transportation, the town became more isolated. "St. Joseph found itself tucked away nearly out of sight to modern travelers," states the narration of a Heart of Louisiana video about the community.[16] The video shows the resurgence of small businesses on the main street, but with only 740 residents according to the 2022 census and a poverty rate over 34 percent, there are quite a few challenges facing the community.[17,18] Over 75 percent of the residents of St. Joe are Black.

The nearby town of Lake Providence, named after the oxbow lake it borders, isn't as isolated as St. Joe, but it also has a high poverty rate at nearly 50 percent.[19,20] Lake Providence is larger than St. Joe, with approximately 3,000 residents, over 80 percent of whom are Black.[21,22]

CNN reporter John D. Sutter traveled to Lake Providence at the behest of readers who described exceptional income inequality.[23]

The journey resulted in his 2013 story, "The Most Unequal Place in America." He reported, "The rich largely live north of the lake and the poor on the south. They go to different churches and attend different schools. They have different friends and work different jobs. . . . Many of the richer people in town own land and run farms that produce corn, cotton and soybeans. Poorer people used to work on those farms, but they've largely been replaced by the Transformer-size machines you see driving along the road during harvest."

Race is at the root of this disparity, Sutter notes. "Land was given to white families in the 1800s, not to blacks," he writes. "The town resisted integration in the 1960s and '70s, and at least one voting rights activist was shot in the parish during that struggle."

In the Deep South, the not-so-distant history of the enslavement of Black people can still feel very present. "You have banks named after plantations, you have Black and White families with the same last names—the history of slavery is never really far away," said Matt Alexander, the mayor of St. Joe at the time we conducted the focus groups, in an interview.

Low health outcomes show how disinvestment of Black communities has affected social and physical mobility, which we can trace directly to enslavement. Wealth is still very much tied to land ownership. "If you want to tie this to arrested mobility," says Alexander, "poor people are marrying poor people, and wealthy people with land are marrying wealthy people with land. So, you're not inching anywhere closer to what you could see as a more equal society. . . . It's probably less."

Black land ownership, which is highly concentrated in the South, decreased from 20 million acres in the early 1900s to between 2 and 7 million acres by the end of the twentieth century.[24] In the agricultural communities of St. Joe and Lake Providence, lack of land ownership is linked to poverty and race.

St. Joe and Lake Providence were chosen for the LSU AgCenter study because they are "high obesity targeted communities" as defined by the Centers for Disease Control and Prevention. Tensas Parish (where St. Joe is located) and East Carroll Parish (where Lake Providence is located), rank 61 and 63, respectively, out of 64 in the state for health outcomes.[25,26] Thirty percent of Tensas residents are obese, 33 percent of adults are inactive, and 19 percent have diabetes.[27] Forty percent of East Carroll residents are obese, 28 percent of adults are inactive, and 14 percent have diabetes.[28] For these rural communities along the Mississippi River, the levee trails could be a great source of recreation and outdoor exploration.

Focus Group Purpose and Structure

My work with the LSU AgCenter was part of a feasibility study to improve the trail and access to it on the west bank of the Mississippi River through the Louisiana Delta parishes. The focus groups were held to help policymakers understand the circumstances and needs of Black residents.

In addition to conducting the focus groups with Black residents from St. Joe and Lake Providence, I summarized the focus groups with the White residents and land owners along the river that were conducted by LSU AgCenter. In those focus groups we heard from thirteen Black residents and sixteen White residents.

"When people think of rural areas, they think of them as hard to reach areas—I think saying that really puts the responsibility on the community or blames the community in a way for not being as accessible as we would like them to be," says Jamila Freightman in an interview. "But I think figuring out ways to actually meet the people where they are and understanding the culture in rural communities in regards to communication and the best ways to reach them . . . is important."

Freightman explains that all of the levees in Louisiana are public property maintained by their local levee boards or municipalities. "Although these laws exist, local rules regarding who actually has permission to access the levee remain unclear," Freightman says. The study by LSU AgCenter used the Social Determinants of Health framework to understand the perceptions of access to outdoor resources for physical activity.

As a reminder, the social determinants of health is a framework used in public health to look at all of the environmental factors in a person's life—where they live, where they work, what they do day-to-day, and their demographics—to determine their ability to maintain a fairly healthy lifestyle.[29] What public health researchers have found is that where someone lives has a huge impact on their ability to be healthy. If someone lives in a location where there are no supermarkets within walking distance, they have less access to healthy foods. And, as we have covered in this book, race is a factor in where someone lives.

In this case, one of the social determinants that is being investigated is the societal rules—written or unwritten—that restrict access to a public space for people based on race.

"The two areas that we focused on were chosen because they have a levee resource or a levee that is accessible from the town center," says Freightman. "There are clear paths that you can walk up to access the top of the levee and walk. In these areas, over half of the population is African-American. One of the parishes has the highest obesity rate. One of the areas was deemed the poorest county in the United States."

Participants in the study were asked questions about how often they are physically active and whether access to public spaces such as trails and parks is easy and safe. They were also asked about whether they felt comfortable and welcome running, biking, or walking on levee trails. What we found wasn't surprising: There was a distinct difference between the responses from White and Black residents.

The Findings

There were a few fears that White and Black respondents shared. One was animals on the levee: snakes, bears, loose dogs, or cows from farms nearby. Another was the lack of lighting, which made the levee feel particularly unsafe at night. Also, there was a lack of clarity on who can use the public levee and when.

"Participants from both groups expressed the need for some type of rules along the levee, so that people know what they can and cannot do," says Freightman. "I think among the Black participants, it felt like the rules are not available possibly on purpose . . . to keep Black people from accessing it."

Black residents expressed a general feeling and discomfort that came from interactions with White residents in the community. They were made to feel that the trail was not for them. "It's like when you go up there, they are looking at you like, 'Why are you here?,'" Freightman said, relaying a response from one participant.

Black respondents in both the Lake Providence and St. Joe groups expressed the feeling that the White residents were overvigilant of their movements. "I just don't go up there because you know they're watching," one of the St. Joe participants said. The fears of the levee and racial profiling also extended into rumors that circulate within the Black community. Specifically in Lake Providence, there was talk of dead bodies being found on the levees. In St. Joe, there was fear of accidentally coming across a land owner's private property, especially one of the farms nearby. The cows that occasionally wandered onto the levee made people feel as if the levee land was an extension of the farmers' land and that these land owners monopolized that public property.

The unwelcomeness extended beyond just a feeling for some Black participants. Some in St. Joe said they'd been asked to leave the levee before, especially when White people were facilitating events or camps.

"Considering the power dynamics and the social segregation that exists in these areas, we know that people with more resources and larger networks probably have a better idea of what they can and cannot do, who owns what land," says Freightman. "Based on the data that we have, the White participants felt a little bit more comfortable or would access the areas anyway, and they didn't feel like anything would happen to them and didn't really have any negative experiences of anyone bothering them when they did access the levee."

The fears of White participants were about not knowing what is private or public property or feeling that the area was unsightly. But none mentioned feeling unwelcome or like they were in danger from other people because they weren't supposed to be there. There was an acknowledgment that the Black and White community members had different experiences. "I think you have two communities here," said one White participant from Lake Providence. "You have those in the community who have access and those that don't."

Many of the Black residents, especially the Lake Providence group, didn't view a lot of the types of activities that could take place on the levee—

walking, bicycling, and jogging—as ones they would associate with exercise rather than transportation. For them, car ownership is seen as a status symbol, and those who bike or walk often do so because they cannot afford a vehicle. St. Joe participants also see these activities more as a necessity for transportation because of limited access to cars.

Similar to Equiticity's work in North Lawndale, the focus groups show that it is not productive to shun travel by car in a mobility campaign. They also found that for Black residents to use the levee, there would need to be encouragement and clarity about access, not just infrastructure improvements.

The findings reveal that while there is a desire for increased physical activity, numerous barriers—economic, safety, and social—restrict the mobility and physical activity of Black residents.

Conclusions and Next Steps

This study was the first step in what will hopefully result in a trail through the 130 miles of the Mississippi River and consideration of how everyone in the community will benefit from it.

Freightman believes that this work is "really bringing attention to the fact that not everyone feels like they can access the community's amenities. Even if they want to go to the lake in St. Joseph, there's Lake Bruin, and a lot of the Black community, they don't feel welcome there. It's similar to certain parts of the lake in Lake Providence. If they wanted to bike around the lake, they don't feel like they can do that. . . . So it's also bringing those perspectives to the forefront."

Although the trail upgrades are uncertain, the partnership with the AgCenter has helped the towns of St. Joe and Lake Providence to leverage grant funding so the trail will be accessible to their communities.

The findings from the levee focus groups highlight how systemic barriers—such as racial discrimination, economic inequalities, and infrastructural deficiencies—restrict the physical activity and mobility of marginalized communities.

Promoting these findings among professionals in the planning, health, environmental, and transportation sectors is crucial because it encourages a more comprehensive and justice-oriented approach to urban and community development. We shared the findings with the Centers for Disease

Control and Prevention, and we shared our work through the *Arrested Mobility* podcast. Although there hasn't been movement by Louisiana to improve the levee, the focus group outcome helps show the level of work that must be done to include the community in that process whenever it does get going. By incorporating the experiences and needs of marginalized communities into planning processes, professionals can work to eliminate the structural inequalities that limit mobility and access.

A COMMUNITY ADVOCATE LEADS MOBILITY JUSTICE LEADERSHIP DEVELOPMENT IN LOS ANGELES

The Southern California Association of Governments (SCAG) has taken an ambitious approach to embedding equity into the culture of the organization, as mentioned in Chapter 4. But what does this look like in action?

SCAG is investing in community-based organizations and, more specifically, in people, who have the potential to help transform the way urban planning is done. Planner and biking enthusiast Yolanda Davis-Overstreet has been able to leverage her work with the help of SCAG. "She's the perfect example," says SCAG's Kome Ajise. As one of sixteen recipients of a SCAG Go Human grant in June 2024, "Davis-Overstreet is helping to bring an awareness of mobility justice to high-fatality corridors in Los Angeles."[30]

But it all started with her love of biking.

Biking While Black

When Yolanda Davis-Overstreet was in her thirties in the 1990s, she discovered the power of biking. This was solidified when she participated in the AIDS/LifeCycle Ride, a 500+-mile, seven-day bike ride from Los Angeles to San Francisco to raise funds for HIV/AIDS organizations.[31] "I think that was instrumental from the standpoint of how amazing bicycling can be from a health perspective as well as a joy perspective, because with a lot of laughing and talking, you know, on this seven-day bike ride that made me come back to my community and say, *man, I want to continue to ride like this*," she said in an interview. She wanted to find people in her Los Angeles community to ride with, but she didn't know many other Black cyclists there. Her love of biking and desire to bring it to her people has driven her work ever since.

In 2011, she started Ride in Living Color, a bicycling advocacy effort dedicated to educating Black community members about mobility justice. Her work on Ride in Living Color is what led her to ask, "Why doesn't my community have bike lanes?" That question, she says, "opened Pandora's box."

To help answer that question, Davis-Overstreet began learning about urban planning and engaging in the Black Lives Matter community events and educational gatherings. She also began researching the history of redlining in her community—the community where her parents purchased their home in 1961. She discovered that her neighborhood, which is now called West Adams, in South Los Angeles, was considered "declining" and was color-coded as "yellow" during the redlining era.

The historic neighborhood of Sugar Hill in Crenshaw, east of where Davis-Overstreet's parents bought their house, was once home to some of the wealthiest Black residents in the city. But Sugar Hill was decimated when it was cut in half to build the I-10 Freeway, also known as the Santa Monica Freeway, which opened in 1961.[32,33]

Davis-Overstreet's journey resulted in a project called Biking While Black, which produced a few short films of the same name that ask whether Black people are safe biking. The first film she produced in 2022, and the companion fifty-two-page guide developed in 2023, were both funded by SCAG. Her work addresses needs and inequalities by focusing on human infrastructure, which is the systems that affect people in a community, including healthcare, childcare, education, and jobs (similar to what Equiticity calls "software"). It's not the physical facilities but the systems in place to ensure that that physical infrastructure serves the community.

She now runs Yolanda Davis-Overstreet Consulting, where she "forms teams to combat these specific human and mobility injustices, disenfranchisement, police harassment, policy, and joy."[34] She helps to convene people and organizations who might not normally sit at the table together, with a goal of building leadership around mobility justice.

In 2020 Davis-Overstreet developed a "curriculum" and convenings of organizations and stakeholders to identify needs for roadway improvements and develop solutions. This work was also funded by SCAG. She later developed a roadmap with recommendations and strategies to "promote equity, safety, and joy in cycling, benefiting both BIPOC communities and the broader society."

Venice Boulevard

In 2024, with the SCAG Go Human grant, Davis-Overstreet's leadership development program looked at creating a model planning and community engagement approach for safety using a high-injury network of streets in a 1-mile radius around Venice Boulevard in the Arlington Heights neighborhood of Los Angeles. Three people were killed in hit-and-run accidents in crosswalks in this area between October and November 2023. Davis-Overstreet and her co-facilitator, Brooke Rios, the principal of three local charter schools, identified the area because it is dangerous, it is near schools, and it is predominantly Latino.[35] Rios was the principal at Davis-Overstreet's daughter's school when they first met, and Davis-Overstreet asked whether she could advocate for a crosswalk on the dangerous intersection in front of the school. After seven years of advocacy, a traffic light and crosswalk were installed in April 2020. Davis-Overstreet and Rios continued working together to develop this mobility justice project to center schools and their surrounding communities.

"Part of the education and engagement work we do is facilitating a platform for community and leaders to share the narratives about how our streets and communities have been designed in such ways that never took into account the wellbeing and safety of Black lives," says Davis-Overstreet. "Once constructed decades ago, our city municipalities never looked back to improve upon the crumbling infrastructures." Davis-Overstreet and Rios want to build a cadre of leaders who use the lens of mobility justice—who understand how history informs the infrastructure of today.

For the Venice Boulevard project, called "Liberating Our Streets," Davis-Overstreet and Rios brought together a core team made up of community members or representatives from community-based organizations to identify improvements. Davis-Overstreet intentionally brought people together who wouldn't normally be collaborating, including public school officials, professionals from city agencies, and the Bus Riders Union. Bringing groups together from different perspectives can be transformative and help everyone envision a way forward that serves the entire community. The project participants had the opportunity to make recommendations for safety improvements right where they live, work, or play. "Each one of these individuals has connections to a larger system," says Davis-Overstreet. "They bring their own internal knowledge, which is intersectional."

First coined by civil rights advocate and scholar Kimberlé Williams Crenshaw, *intersectionality* means looking at overlapping identities and how they might affect someone's experience of a system.[36] For example, I'm looking primarily at the experiences of arrested mobility of Black Americans in this book. But as I noted, the oppression might be even greater for a Black trans woman because of her overlapping identities as both Black *and* trans.

Davis-Overstreet believes having an intersectional focus helps the core team think more broadly and more creatively about strategies to unarrest the mobility of people in their community, especially the most marginalized.

For the project, Davis-Overstreet and Rios facilitated weekly meetings of at least two hours for six weeks with the core team. The goal was to work through a mobility justice roadmap at these convenings and through field visits to the study area: West Adams, Mid-City, and Arlington Heights, all predominantly Black and Latino neighborhoods.

The goal of the program wasn't necessarily to see that the general recommendations from the team were acted upon; rather, it was an educational process where the cohort was trained in carrying out their work through the lens of mobility justice. Venice Boulevard was their case study. The findings and recommendations from each participant were presented for discussion at the Council District 10 office. Recommendations ranged from improving the bike share system to enhancing the pedestrian infrastructure by the schools in Arlington Heights, which accommodate approximately 1,200 students. The exercise helped participants practice bringing their narrative of living, working, and playing in a community together with data and observations they made throughout the workshop series (Figure 5-2).

Davis-Overstreet sees this work as "expanding mobility justice messaging and cultivating advocates and ambassadors in each community. Our primary goal is to maintain open communication with cohort members to sustain the collaborative work we've developed."

Davis-Overstreet sees the six-week "Liberating Our Streets" program, made possible by the SCAG GoHuman grant, as a stepping stone to a larger mobility justice leadership program that would run at least six months to

108 ARRESTED MOBILITY

FIGURE 5-2 The team conducted a walk audit along Washington Boulevard and Burnside Avenue in Los Angeles to see where problems were in order to suggest solutions. This was a breakthrough session for the group, according to Yolanda Davis-Overstreet. (Image courtesy of Yolanda Davis-Overstreet)

allow the cohort to more fully engage with how these injustices affect their lives and their communities.

SCAG's funding of Davis-Overstreet's work is an example of how a municipal planning organization can support mobility justice through leadership development.

FIGHTING AGAINST STOP-AND-FRISK IN THE COURTS IN NEW YORK

In 2014, Lance Rodriguez, whom the police described as "Hispanic," was riding a bike around Queens, New York, when he was stopped by police.[37] The police searched Rodriguez without having reasonable suspicion to do so and found that he had a gun on him. He was arrested and charged with criminal possession of a weapon. At the trial, his defense attorney argued that the officer did not have probable cause to stop him. The judge said that since Rodriguez was on a bike, the officer didn't need probable cause. The officer needed only reasonable suspicion that Rodriguez was armed to stop him.

Rodriguez was sentenced to two years in prison and one year and a half postrelease supervision.[38]

The issue is not that Rodriguez was carrying a weapon illegally but the fact that the police were empowered to pull him over without cause because he was on a bike. If he had been in a car, the officer would have needed probable cause that he was engaged in a criminal activity to pull him over.

In New York, Black and Latino cyclists make up roughly half of the city's cycling population, yet they receive a disproportionate number of tickets for minor infractions compared with their White counterparts.[39] Such practices not only disrupt the daily lives of people like Rodriguez but also contribute to a broader environment of fear and mistrust between communities of color and law enforcement.

Although this troubling pattern is not isolated to New York, laws in New York made it easier for police to stop without cause. Under the Bloomberg administration, the New York Police Department (NYPD) stop-and-frisk program allowed police to detain and search people if they had reasonable suspicion of a crime. The NYPD stopped nearly 700,000 people in 2011, at the height of this practice. Most of them were Black and Latino men and boys.[40]

In 2013, the NYPD's widespread application of stop-and-frisk was found by the courts to be unconstitutional.[41] However stop-and-frisk didn't stop completely. The number of stops reported in New York went down, but the practice continued, as evidenced by Lance Rodriguez's arrest.

In 2022, the New York Civil Liberties Union (NYCLU), my consulting firm, and other partners submitted an amicus brief to the New York Court of Appeals to address the unconstitutional practices of racially biased police stops of cyclists. This case, covered in depth on my podcast *Arrested Mobility*, is a compelling example of how targeted advocacy and legal action can challenge and potentially dismantle systems that disproportionately criminalize communities of color.[42]

The amicus brief argued that police stops of moving bicycles, like those of motor vehicles, should be considered seizures requiring reasonable suspicion of unlawful activity. Lowering this standard would give law enforcement excessive discretion, exacerbating the racial disparities in policing practices. The brief underscored that unchecked discretion has historically led to discriminatory practices, such as New York's notorious stop-and-frisk policy, disproportionately targeting Black and Latino communities.

The Arguments and Key Findings

The amicus brief made three key arguments. The first was that requiring a lower constitutional standard for cyclists will increase rampant racial profiling of Black and Brown cyclists by the police. "Here we argue that extensive research shows that when police officers have more discretion, they aggressively and disproportionately target communities of color," says Daniel Lambright, senior staff attorney for the NYCLU. Data from the NYPD and other sources reveal a stark racial bias in how cyclists are policed. Black and Latino cyclists are disproportionately stopped, searched, and ticketed, often without reasonable cause. In Chicago, 56 percent of all bike tickets were issued in predominantly Black neighborhoods and only 18 percent in White neighborhoods.[43] In Long Beach, Black cyclists were 3.5 times more likely to be stopped on their bike than White cyclists.[44] And in New York City, 75 percent of tickets in the first nine months of 2021 were issued to Black and Latino people.[45]

The second argument is that allowing police officers to pull over and stop cyclists without reasonable suspicion risks alienating communities of color from participating in biking, which in turn has an effect on public health. Unjustified police stops deter people of color from cycling, a mode of transport that offers numerous health and environmental benefits. By impeding access to safe and equitable transportation options, these practices contribute to broader systemic inequities in health and mobility.

"It's incredibly humiliating to be called to spread eagle and stand against the wall while an officer looks through and touches all parts of your body," says Lambright. "That's the type of harassment that actually prevents people of color and alienates people of color from biking. We want to obviously encourage Black and Brown people to engage in biking, and we want to encourage everyone to engage in biking. . . . A ruling from the court saying that people on bikes have less protection from police harassment counters that encouragement."

The third argument is that police stops of moving bicycles significantly interfere with cyclist freedom of movement and therefore constitute seizures requiring reasonable suspicion. The ruling affirms that all road users, whether cyclists or motorists, are entitled to constitutional protections against unreasonable searches and seizures.

"The reason that cars are held to a higher standard is because courts have held that stopping cars creates a significant intrusion on the freedom of movement of people driving vehicles," says Lambright. "In this portion of the argument, we argue that officers pulling over a cyclist creates as serious and as significant an interruption of their liberty as they would for a car driver. This is based on the fact that cyclists on roadways can move just as fast as cars and stop and go traffic and being pulled over by police officers would require a significant amount of energy to safely stop and would significantly intrude upon the cyclist's freedom of movement."

The goal of filing the amicus brief was to show that there are racial implications from the court's ruling. "They cannot just view their rulings, they cannot view criminal justice matters apart from the racial ramifications of their actions and the racial realities of policing," says Lambright.

The case succeeded, and in November 2023, the New York Court of Appeals ruled in favor of the amendment that says that police cannot pull over anyone without probable cause, whether they're on foot or two wheels.[46]

Other Stop-and-Frisk Cases

In 2012, the NYCLU along with Bronx Defenders and Latino Justice brought a lawsuit challenging stop-and-frisk at buildings enrolled in Trespass Affidavit Program (TAP), in which the NYPD was given authority by landlords and owners to patrol private buildings.[47,48] Under TAP, initiated by the NYPD, police officers can enter buildings enrolled in the program and patrol the interior of buildings, including hallways, stairwells, and other common areas and to deter unauthorized people from entering and remaining in these spaces.

"What was happening was kind of in and around those buildings, officers were just stopping Black and Brown men with no suspicion whatsoever because they were near the buildings because they were Black or Brown, frisking them in a very aggressive manner," says Lambright.

In the lawsuit, the plaintiffs argued that the NYPD's use of stop-and-frisk in TAP-enrolled buildings resulted in unconstitutional stops and searches based on race or ethnicity rather than reasonable suspicion of criminal activity. This lawsuit highlighted the risks of granting police unchecked authority in private buildings and the potential for racial profiling and violations of civil rights.

The NYCLU got preliminary injunctions from the federal court in 2012, which required the NYPD to stop this practice.[49] "This case implicated a lot of the issues that we've always cared about, and that I've cared about as a litigator, and really allowed us to talk about stops and the racial effects of that," says Lambright.

TAP still existed on the books, despite the injunction, but was quietly shut down by the NYPD in 2020. Nonetheless, a federal monitor says that as of 2023 the practice of police patrolling inside private buildings still occurs.[50] Banning such practices can only go so far, but it's a step toward holding police departments accountable.

By challenging these laws, the NYLCU is, in effect, challenging the societal *notion* of crime. "Officers often use this kind of phrase, 'high-crime neighborhood,' and they use that to justify doing more invasive actions on people. And in actuality, the data and the research show that high crime areas really just means minority area," says Lambright.

A Call to Action

These cases are powerful examples of how targeted legal advocacy, community engagement, and public awareness can lead to meaningful change. They demonstrate that the fight against arrested mobility—the systemic restriction of movement and access for people of color—not only is possible but can yield substantial victories.

Of course, this doesn't mean that stops won't continue to happen. But police practices must continue to be challenged, whether through the court or through legislation.

I urge bicycle advocates, health professionals, safety experts, and transportation professionals across the country to undertake a comprehensive review of their own state, county, and municipal policies. By critically examining local practices and advocating for policies that require reasonable suspicion for stops of all road users, we can protect the rights of cyclists and ensure that policing practices do not reinforce racial disparities.[51]

These cases serve as a rallying point for advocates across the country to continue the fight for racial justice and mobility equity, ensuring that everyone, regardless of race, has the right to move freely and safely within their communities.

ADVANCING THE MITIGATION OF ARRESTED MOBILITY THROUGH QUALITATIVE RESEARCH

Qualitative research plays a critical role in understanding and addressing the systemic issues contributing to arrested mobility. Equiticity's Go Hub project came as a direct response to the 2021 study they conducted with researchers from the University of Illinois and the Metropolitan Planning Council.[52] They were able to use the results from the focus groups to design a project in partnership with community. The project with the LSU AgCenter provided insight about who feels welcome using public spaces. In order for any kind of improvement along the levee trail system to benefit *all* local community members, they needed to listen to the people who are often least listened to. Yolanda Davis-Overstreet is empowering community leaders to use their narratives and those of the people in their communities as a basis for a qualitative look at what improvements need to be made.

Other studies that I've led over the years, such as the "Barriers to Biking" report funded by PeopleForBikes[53] and "Bicycling Among Black and Latino Women" and "Barriers to Bicycle Access and Use in Black and Hispanic Communities," both funded by the New Jersey Department of Transportation during my time at Rutgers,[54,55] highlight the importance of qualitative insights in uncovering the lived experiences of these communities and formulating effective, community-centric interventions.

These studies were conducted in a pre–George Floyd era, when racial inequities in policing and mobility were less widely acknowledged or discussed. The willingness of these institutions to engage with these challenging topics demonstrates a forward-thinking approach and a dedication to fostering equitable access to transportation and public spaces. By supporting and expanding these efforts, agencies such as PeopleForBikes can play a pivotal role in driving national conversations and policy changes aimed at dismantling the systemic barriers that restrict mobility for people of color.

By delving into the personal narratives, perceptions, and daily realities of residents, qualitative research provides a nuanced understanding of the barriers to mobility and helps shape policies and programs that are more responsive to the needs of those most affected.

Qualitative research allows policymakers, transportation planners, and advocates to

- **Identify root causes** that quantitative data alone might miss, by capturing the voices of those most affected. It reveals the social and psychological barriers, such as fear of racial violence or cultural stigmatization of biking, that are critical to address.
- **Tailor interventions** to the needs and preferences of marginalized communities. For example, understanding that Black and Latino women fear harassment while biking can lead to targeted safety programs and community policing reforms that directly address these concerns.
- **Promote community-centric solutions** by involving community members in the planning and implementation of mobility solutions. Programs that are co-designed with residents are more likely to be culturally relevant, well received, and sustainable.
- **Support policy reform** through powerful narratives. For example, the stories of residents facing racial profiling or lacking access to safe infrastructure can be compelling evidence for policymakers to prioritize investments in equitable transportation infrastructure and revise discriminatory policing practices.

A Call to Action for Transportation Professionals

To effectively address arrested mobility and promote equitable access to transportation, it is crucial for researchers, planners, engineers, and policymakers to integrate qualitative research into their efforts. The insights gained from the studies supported by PeopleForBikes and New Jersey Department of Transportation provide a roadmap for understanding the unique challenges faced by marginalized communities and developing targeted, community-driven solutions. By centering the voices and experiences of those most affected, we can work toward dismantling systemic barriers and ensuring that everyone has the freedom and opportunity to move safely and confidently within their communities.

Promoting these research findings among transportation professionals, health advocates, and policymakers is essential to fostering a more just and inclusive transportation landscape nationwide.

BEYOND THE CASE STUDIES

What this chapter shows is that the work of un-arresting mobility can be done from multiple avenues, in communities all over the United States.

There are so many creative possibilities to un-arrest the mobility of Black Americans, and I'm eager to hear more from those of you reading this book.

Conclusion

Breaking the Silence

"Our lives begin to end the day we become silent about things that matter."
—Martin Luther King Jr.

"Nothing is as central to America's cultural DNA as freedom," wrote Elaine Kamarck and William A. Galston of the Brookings Institution after the freedom-themed 2024 Democratic National Convention. "After all, we as a nation were born out of a desire for freedom from King George."[1] How those freedoms are upheld might differ between the political parties, but the concept remains almost holy to most Americans. But are all Americans truly free?

When I think of the idea of freedom, I think of mobility. Mobility is an area where our country has not lived up to its promise of freedom for all. Certainly, there has been progress since the time of enslavement. Through the resilience and resistance of Black people, there have been successes. But freedom of movement is still denied to Black Americans, as shown throughout this book.

Of course, systemic racism and arrested mobility are not confined to the United States.

In 1948, the United Nations drafted a Universal Declaration of Human Rights, in which freedom of movement is stated as a universal human right:

1. *Everyone has the right to freedom of movement and residence within the borders of each state.*
2. *Everyone has the right to leave any country, including his own, and to return to his country.*[2]

I'm not sure that there is a place in the world where these declarations are followed. There are places where these rights are explicitly violated, such as in Afghanistan, where the Taliban forbids women from leaving their homes or traveling without being accompanied by a male relative or chaperone.[3] But in most places, the arrested mobility of marginalized peoples happens imperceptibly to those who are not directly affected.

The example that follows is from Canada, to show similarities to the many examples in the book from the United States. My colleague at the University of Manitoba, Orly Linovski, analyzed policing of cyclists in Winnipeg between 2018 and 2020.[4] She found that the hundreds of tickets issued for "failing to exercise due care" or riding on the sidewalk were in neighborhoods where there weren't very many safe bike routes. "The huge differences in where tickets are issued—primarily in low-income and racialized communities—means it is critical that these neighbourhoods are prioritized for investments that make cycling safer," she wrote.[5] In 2015, the city created an award-winning cycling and pedestrian strategy that focused on equity, yet Linovski observed that the majority of areas identified in the strategy as having higher needs received no new bike investments.

I could have chosen an example from just about anywhere in the world, as the need to un-arrest the mobility of Black people is universal, even in predominantly Black countries, nations, and communities. Nowhere is exempt. This demonstrates the importance of seeing this issue as thematic as opposed to episodic. Thus, no matter where you are in the world or what your position is to affect change, you have a role to play in un-arresting the mobility of Black people, people of color, and the most marginalized people in your communities through five general guidelines to un-arrest mobility.

GUIDELINES TO UN-ARREST MOBILITY

These guidelines for un-arresting mobility could be thought of as frameworks of mobility justice or racial justice—the concepts are essentially the same. Using an equity framework is about understanding the procedures and processes in the distribution of resources and then addressing the root causes of the problem. These guidelines walk you through the process.

Recognize and Diagnose the Problem

The first step is to assess the presence of arrested mobility for your community or district.

Some of this information will be data driven and some will be gathered by listening to community members, specifically those who are historically overlooked.

Analyze traffic safety data, income disparities, and enforcement trends and patterns such as data found in Mapping Police Violence.[6] Overlay these findings with racial and demographic data to see who is most affected. Additionally, this analysis should consider intersectionality, ensuring that various identity factors (e.g., race, gender, disability) are considered in unarresting mobility. Look at where investments are being made—and, more importantly, where they are not. And then listen to community members whose neighborhoods are not being invested in to hear what they want and need.

SCAG did this type of analysis in their baseline report, mentioned in Chapter 4.[7] They analyzed data and diagnosed a lack of investment in communities of color. By diagnosing the problem, they can see where they fell short before and where they needed to invest their efforts.

And of course, the data and analysis should be accessible to the community. Not only should it be posted on the website, but there should be corresponding outreach campaigns to guide community members to the information.

Acknowledge Historical and Ongoing Barriers

It is important to learn about the historical context of the community or district to understand the root of current issues. Whether it's redlining, highway construction that displaced Black communities, or discriminatory housing practices, these are not relics of the past—they continue to limit mobility today. Learn from this history to inform solutions that are restorative and reparative.

This context must be heard, understood, and integrated into the next steps for repair.

Identify Causes of Arrested Mobility

Once you understand how mobility is being arrested and you have learned about the history and the context of the community, look at the causes. In many cases, it's not going to be any one challenge but layers of them. Examine the systemic barriers that restrict mobility. These may include discriminatory policing and policies, lack of access to reliable transportation, economic disenfranchisement, and environmental injustices. The arrested mobility of Black people is not just one issue but the culmination of many intersecting inequities.

For example, Equiticity found that in the North Lawndale neighborhood in Chicago mobility was arrested by years of economic disenfranchisement and lack of investment from the city, including cuts to transit service.

Involve the Community in Solutions

Involve the community in every step of the process, from diagnosing the problem to designing and implementing solutions. Top-down approaches often fail because they do not consider the lived experiences of those most affected.

In the case of The Go Hub, the community was involved in defining the problem through paid community advisory board members and then through focus groups and design charrettes.

Community input is not only valuable—it is essential to the success of any mobility justice initiative.

Ensure Sustainability and Accountability

Implementing solutions is not enough; they must be sustained and continuously evaluated to ensure they are working as intended. Mechanisms must be established for accountability, ensuring that communities continue to benefit from the investments. This includes going back to the community regularly to identify whether a project is meeting their needs, asking what is working, and what could make it better.

For example, when SCAG published their "Racial Equity Early Action Plan" in May 2021, they committed to having each department report on the work that they did each quarter to show how they had implemented the goals.[8] That accountability led to a wholesale culture change within the organization. After three years, the quarterly reports were no longer necessary because the process of community engagement was second nature. That's not to say that's where the work stopped. Rather, it just meant that SCAG leveled up and came up with ways to more effectively and equitably work with community-based organizations. This work will require another level of accountability.

Accountability should be built into the structural maintenance of the engineering and design of a project. It will help to ensure that any unintended consequences are addressed quickly. Long-term change requires not just action but sustained commitment.

WE ALL HAVE A ROLE TO UN-ARREST MOBILITY

One of the most important takeaways from this book is that all of us—you, me, your colleagues, your community members—can have a part in un-arresting mobility. And the first step for many of us is to *not* be silent.

Dr. King's words from the epigraph serve as a reminder that silence, particularly in the face of injustice, is not an option. As planners, engineers, health professionals, advocates, and those responsible for shaping the future of our communities, we have a profound responsibility to confront the systemic inequities that persist in our fields. The arrested mobility of Black people in America and around the world demands not just our attention but our immediate action. We must break our silence.

Many of us entered our professions with the noble intention to improve lives. Even if our academic institutions failed to fully equip us to confront racial disparities, deep down, I believe this truth remains in our hearts: We chose this work to help all people. It's easy to lose sight of this when systems, structures, and routines become the norm. But we cannot afford complacency. We are called to be more than technicians or administrators; we must be advocates for justice.

For those among us who share a connection to the Abrahamic faiths—Christianity, Judaism, Islam—the directive is clear: love thy neighbor as thyself. Black people, too often excluded from the promise of equitable treatment, are part of this moral commandment. It is not enough to admire Dr. King's dream from a distance. We are the ones he dreamed about. Our moral compass was defined before many of us were born, and it points us toward a just society for all.

This fight is about more than just Black lives—it is about the future of this nation. The United States is rapidly becoming a majority-minority country. We are standing at a crossroads, and we can either embrace this diversity and forge a path toward freedom and justice, or we can continue to perpetuate the mass incarceration, both physical and metaphorical, of Black bodies and Black potential. The alarming rates at which Black men and women are arrested and incarcerated is a statistic we should all be ashamed of—and one that demands action, not just reflection.

If you are not Black, and you do not stand up to fight for your Black neighbors, colleagues, friends, and, in some cases, family members, know this: Black people have a long, unshakable history of resilience. We will continue to push this country toward justice—for our sake and for the sake of the world, as we always have. But where will you stand in this historic moment? Will you help dismantle the systems that perpetuate arrested mobility, or will you stand by and watch history pass you by?

As a veteran, I know what it means to sacrifice for freedom. I served with the full awareness that I might have to lay down my life for this country. How could I now abandon the fight for freedom in exchange for comfort or a paycheck? I won't. This battle is far from over, and I am fully committed to it.

But this is not about me.

The urgency is supreme. This is our fight, and I call on each and every one of you to rise to the occasion. To remain silent is to be complicit. To act is to be part of a movement that will change not just our profession but our country, and indeed, the world.

This is a fight for justice, dignity, and freedom of movement for all. The time to act is now.

And although it may be true that, as Alejandro Jodorowsky said, "Birds born in a cage think flying is an illness," I say, "Fly anyway!"

NOTES

FOREWORD

1. District of Columbia, Maternal Mortality Review Committee (DC MMRC), "2019–2020 Annual Report," https://ocme.dc.gov/sites/default/files/dc/sites/ocme/agency_content/Maternal%20Mortality%20Review%20Committee%20Annual%20Report_Finalv2.pdf.
2. David D. Kirkpatrick, Steve Eder, Kim Barker, and Julie Tate, "Why Many Police Traffic Stops Turn Deadly," *The New York Times*, October 31, 2021, https://www.nytimes.com/2021/10/31/us/police-traffic-stops-killings.html.
3. David Leonhardt, "What Groups Need Affirmative Action," *The New York Times*, March 15, 2024, https://www.nytimes.com/2024/03/15/briefing/affirmative-action.html.

INTRODUCTION

1. Oregon Secretary of State, *Black in Oregon: A Timeline of Black History*, Oregon State Archives, https://sos.oregon.gov/archives/exhibits/black-history/Pages/context/chronology.aspx (accessed September 24, 2024).
2. Kristine de Leon, "Is Portland Still the Whitest Big City in America?" *OregonLive*, last modified October 7, 2022, https://www.oregonlive.com/data/2022/10/is-portland-still-the-whitest-big-city-in-america.html.
3. Jonathan Levinson, "Portland Has 5th Worst Arrest Disparities in the Nation, According to Data," *OPB*, last modified February 7, 2021, https://www.opb.org/article/2021/02/07/portland-has-5th-worst-arrest-disparities-in-the-nation-according-to-data/.
4. Conrad Wilson, "Jeremy Christian Sentenced to 2 Life Terms in Prison for 2017 MAX Stabbings," *OPB*, last modified June 24, 2020, https://www.opb.org/news/article/jeremy-christian-sentencing-hearing-victim-impact-statements-portland-oregon/.

5. Amelia Templeton, "Earlier Releases Surface for Man Charged with Stabbing Black Teens on Portland MAX Train," *OPB*, last modified September 12, 2023, https://www.opb.org/article/2023/09/12/earlier-releases-man-charged-with-stabbing-black-teens-portland-max-train/.
6. National Community Reinvestment Coalition, "Shifting Neighborhoods: Gentrification and Cultural Displacement in Portland, OR," *NCRC*, https://ncrc.org/gentrification-portlandor/ (accessed September 24, 2024).
7. Portland Bureau of Transportation, "High Crash Network Streets and Intersections," Portland.gov, https://www.portland.gov/transportation/vision-zero/high-crash-network-streets-and-intersections (accessed September 24, 2024).
8. Charles Brown et al., PeopleForBikes, *Barriers to Biking: Exploring the Needs and Experiences of BIPOC and White People Who Want to Ride Bikes*, July 2020, https://prismic-io.s3.amazonaws.com/peopleforbikes/6b4cc95b-295d-4947-88fb-839702944c97_PFB-Final-Barriers+to+Biking+REPORT.pdf (accessed September 24, 2024).
9. Ibid., 98.
10. "Portland's Bike Share Program," *BIKETOWN*, https://biketownpdx.com/ (accessed September 24, 2024).
11. In 2019, BIKETOWN was among ten city bike share systems in a study I conducted with a team from Rutgers University, The State University of New Jersey, and the New Jersey Bicycle and Pedestrian Resource Center looking at where docking stations were placed relative to the socioeconomic makeup of a community and the demographics of who has access to the program.
12. Alan M. Voorhees Transportation Center, "Bike Share in New Jersey: Where Do We Stand?," Rutgers University, February 11, 2020, https://njbikeped.org/wp-content/uploads/2022/09/Bike-Share_02-11-2020_sm.pdf (accessed September 24, 2024).
13. Ibid., 11.
14. Ibid., 51.
15. Since then, BIKETOWN has continued to make efforts to center equity not just in where docking stations are placed but also in making the program accessible to people of all income levels through their Biketown For All program, which offers free membership, subsidized ride credits, and low-cost parking on public racks. By 2024, 59 percent of BIKETOWN's trips were made by participants in the equity program. This kind of approach, driven by data and focused on equity, shows that cities can begin to undo the harm caused by centuries of racial exclusion.
16. Beverly Daniel Tatum, *Why Are All the Black Kids Sitting Together in the Cafeteria? And Other Conversations About Race*, Twentieth Anniversary Edition (New York: Basic Books, 2017).
17. Ibid., 86.

18. Matthew A. Raifman and Ernani F. Choma, *Study on Black Americans' Mortality Rates per Mile of Travel* (Boston: Boston University School of Public Health and Harvard T.H. Chan School of Public Health, 2022).
19. Ibid., 163.
20. "Documenting Police Violence in the United States," Police Violence Report, https://policeviolencereport.org/ (accessed September 24, 2024).
21. US Bureau of Labor Statistics, "Unemployment Statistics by Race (2023–2024)," https://www.bls.gov/web/empsit/cpsee_e16.htm (accessed September 21, 2024).
22. National Center for Education Statistics (NCES), "High School Graduation Rates for 2021–2022," US Department of Education, Institute of Education Sciences, https://nces.ed.gov/programs/coe/indicator/coi (accessed September 21, 2024).
23. C. Mandler, "Murders of Trans People Nearly Doubled over Past 4 Years, and Black Trans Women Are Most at Risk, Report Finds," CBS News, October 23, 2022, https://www.cbsnews.com/news/transgender-community-murder-rates-everytown-for-gun-safety-report/ (accessed September 21, 2024).
24. Richard Rothstein, *The Color of Law: A Forgotten History of How Our Government Segregated America* (New York: Liveright Publishing, 2017).
25. Nikhil Anil Patel et al., "Racial/Ethnic Disparities and Determinants of Sufficient Physical Activity Levels," *Kansas Journal of Medicine* no. 15 (August 2022): 267–72, https://doi.org/10.17161/kjm.vol15.17592.
26. Centers for Disease Control and Prevention, *Statistics on Heart Disease Among Black Americans* (Washington, DC: CDC, 2024), https://www.cdc.gov/nchs/fastats/black-health.htm (accessed September 21, 2024).
27. Centers for Disease Control and Prevention, "Why Is Addressing Social Determinants of Health Important?" CDC.gov, last modified October 21, 2021, https://www.cdc.gov/about/priorities/why-is-addressing-sdoh-important.html.
28. Sarah Seo, *Policing the Open Road: How Cars Transformed American Freedom* (Cambridge: Harvard University Press, 2019), 7–8, Kindle.
29. Ibid., vii.
30. Ibid., vii.
31. Ibid., vii.

CHAPTER 1

1. Nadra Kareem Nittle, "What Is Internalized Racism?" *ThoughtCo*, March 1, 2021, https://www.thoughtco.com/what-is-internalized-racism-2834958 (accessed September 24, 2024).
2. Juan Del Toro and Ming-Te Wang, "Racial Bias in School Discipline: Disparities in Suspensions and Expulsions," *American Psychologist* 76, no. 3 (2021): 180.

3. Juan Del Toro and Ming-Te Wang, "For Black Students, Unfairly Harsh Discipline Can Lead to Lower Grades," *American Psychological Association*, October 7, 2021, https://www.apa.org/news/press/releases/2021/10/black-students-harsh-discipline (accessed October 3, 2024).
4. Fran Kritz, "Doctors Often Fail to Listen to Black Mothers, Complicating Births, Survey Finds," *California Health Report*, September 20, 2018, https://www.calhealthreport.org/2018/09/20/doctors-often-fail-listen-black-mothers-complicating-births-survey-finds/ (accessed October 3, 2024).
5. Serena Williams, "What My Life-Threatening Experience Taught Me About Giving Birth," CNN, February 20, 2018, https://www.cnn.com/2018/02/20/opinions/protect-mother-pregnancy-williams-opinion/index.html (accessed October 3, 2024).
6. Frank Batten School of Leadership and Public Policy, "Batten Expert Chats: 'Racial Bias and Healthcare' with Sophie Trawalter," YouTube, June 24, 2020, timestamp 13:37, https://www.youtube.com/watch?v=1YaHkjNWCjg&list=PLjZn10PE0qnlGbcsNHz9h0AVIYomS30qx&index=14 (accessed September 24, 2024).
7. Christopher Mele, "Army Lifts Ban on Dreadlocks for Black Servicewomen," *New York Times*, February 10, 2017, https://www.nytimes.com/2017/02/10/us/army-ban-on-dreadlocks-black-servicewomen.html (accessed September 24, 2024).
8. Nancy A. Heitzeg, "'Whiteness,' criminality, and the double standards of deviance/social control," *Contemporary Justice Review* 18, no. 2 (2013): 197–214, https://doi.org/10.1080/10282580.2015.1025630, 23.
9. Del Toro and Wang, "Racial Bias in School Discipline."
10. Heitzeg, "Whiteness," 26.
11. David Brancaccio, Rose Conlon, and Daniel Shin, "New Research Shows Racial Discrimination in Hiring Is Still Happening at the Earliest Stages," *Marketplace*, August 3, 2021, https://www.marketplace.org/2021/08/03/new-research-shows-racial-discrimination-in-hiring-is-still-happening-at-the-earliest-stages/ (accessed September 24, 2024).
12. Heitzeg, 14.
13. "Noxubee County," Mississippi Parents Campaign, https://msparentscampaign.org/noxubee-county/ (accessed September 24, 2024).
14. Torsheta Jackson, "Private Schools Can Receive Public ARPA Funds," *Mississippi Free Press*, May 2, 2024, https://www.mississippifreepress.org/private-schools-can-receive-public-arpa-funds-mississippi-supreme-court-rules/ (accessed September 24, 2024).
15. Emma Brown, "The Overwhelming Whiteness of U.S. Private Schools," *Washington Post*, March 29, 2016, https://www.washingtonpost.com/news/education

/wp/2016/03/29/the-overwhelming-whiteness-of-u-s-private-schools-in-six-maps-and-charts/ (accessed September 24, 2024).
16. The White House, "Justice 40 Initiative," https://www.whitehouse.gov/environmentaljustice/justice40/ (accessed October 3, 2024).
17. Logan Schmidt, Micah Haskell-Hoehl, and Hayne Yoon, "Target 2020: Police Violence by the Numbers," *Vera*, July 7, 2020, https://www.vera.org/news/target-2020/data-backed-outrage-police-violence-by-the-numbers (accessed September 24, 2024).
18. Stanford Open Policing Project, "Findings on Racial Disparities," https://openpolicing.stanford.edu/findings/ (accessed September 24, 2024).
19. Reed T. DeAngelis, "Systemic Racism in Police Killings: New Evidence from the Mapping Police Violence Database, 2013–2021," *Race and Justice* 14, no. 3 (July 2024): 413, https://doi.org/10.1177/21533687211047943 (accessed September 25, 2024).
20. Ashley Nellis, "The Color of Justice: Racial and Ethnic Disparity in State Prisons," *Sentencing Project*, October 12, 2021, https://www.sentencingproject.org/reports/the-color-of-justice-racial-and-ethnic-disparity-in-state-prisons-the-sentencing-project/ (accessed September 24, 2024).
21. Nazgol Ghandnoosh and Celeste Berry, "One in Five: Disparities in Crime and Policing," *The Sentencing Project*, November 2, 2023, https://www.sentencingproject.org/reports/one-in-five-disparities-in-crime-and-policing/ (accessed October 3, 2024).
22. Gillian B. White, "Why Black Workers Really Do Need to Be Twice as Good," *The Atlantic*, October 2015, https://www.theatlantic.com/business/archive/2015/10/why-black-workers-really-do-need-to-be-twice-as-good/409276/.
23. Scott Winship et al., "Long Shadows: The Black–White Gap in Multigenerational Poverty," Brookings, June 10, 2021, https://www.brookings.edu/articles/long-shadows-the-black-white-gap-in-multigenerational-poverty/ (accessed September 24, 2024).
24. Candace Jackson, "What Is Redlining?" *New York Times*, August 17, 2021, https://www.nytimes.com/2021/08/17/realestate/what-is-redlining.html (accessed October 1, 2024).
25. Greg Miller, "Maps Show How Tearing Down City Slums Displaced Thousands," *National Geographic*, December 15, 2017, https://www.nationalgeographic.com/history/article/urban-renewal-projects-maps-united-states?loggedin=true&rnd=1699473473817 (accessed September 24, 2024).
26. Hollis Lynch, "African American Life During the Great Depression and the New Deal," *Encyclopedia Britannica*, last updated October 4, 2024, https://www.britannica.com/topic/African-American/African-American-life-during-the-Great-Depression-and-the-New-Deal.

27. Richard Rothstein, *The Color of Law: A Forgotten History of How Our Government Segregated America* (New York: Liveright, 2017), 63–4.
28. Rashawn Ray et al., "Homeownership, Racial Segregation, and Policies for Racial Wealth Equity," *Brookings*, September 1, 2021, https://www.brookings.edu/articles/homeownership-racial-segregation-and-policies-for-racial-wealth-equity/ (accessed September 24, 2024).
29. Melanie Hanson, "Student Loan Debt by Race," *Education Data Initiative*, last updated May 12, 2024, https://educationdata.org/student-loan-debt-by-race (accessed September 24, 2024).
30. Liam Reynolds, Vanessa G. Perry, and Jung Hyun Choi, "Closing the Homeownership Gap Will Require Rooting Systemic Racism Out of Mortgage Underwriting," *The Urban Institute*, October 12, 2021, https://www.urban.org/urban-wire/closing-homeownership-gap-will-require-rooting-systemic-racism-out-mortgage-underwriting (accessed September 24, 2024).
31. Michelle Aronowitz, Edward L. Golding, and Jung Hyun Choi, "*The Unequal Costs of Black Homeownership*," MIT Golub Center for Finance and Policy, September 17, 2020, https://mitsloan.mit.edu/centers-initiatives/mit-gcfp/unequal-costs-black-homeownership (accessed October 2, 2024).
32. Leila Morsy and Richard Rothstein, *Toxic Stress and Children in Poverty: Causes and Policy Solutions* (Washington, DC: Economic Policy Institute, 2016), 18, https://www.epi.org/publication/toxic-stress-and-childrens-outcomes-african-american-children-growing-up-poor-are-at-greater-risk-of-disrupted-physiological-functioning-and-depressed-academic-achievement/ (accessed September 21, 2024).
33. Valentina Lagomarsino, "Racism, Toxic Stress, and Education Policy," *Science in the News*, Harvard Medical School, October 24, 2020, https://sitn.hms.harvard.edu/flash/2020/racism-toxic-stress-and-education-policy/ (accessed September 24, 2024).
34. Adewale A. Maye, "The Myth of Race-Neutral Policy," *Economic Policy Institute*, June 15, 2022, https://www.epi.org/publication/the-myth-of-race-neutral-policy/ (accessed September 24, 2024).
35. Jeannie Suk Gersen, "After Affirmative Action Ends," *New Yorker*, June 26, 2023, https://www.newyorker.com/news/daily-comment/after-affirmative-action-ends (accessed September 24, 2024).
36. Adewale A. Maye, "The Myth of Race-Neutral Policy."
37. Triesta Fowler and Monica Webb Hooper, "It Takes a Village: Community Support and Health Among Black Youth," *Musings from the Mezzanine*, National Library of Medicine, February 23, 2023, https://nlmdirector.nlm.nih.gov/2023/02/23/it-takes-a-village-community-support-and-the-fortification-of-health-among-black-or-african-american-youth/ (accessed September 24, 2024).

38. Robert Taylor et al., "Fictive Kin Networks Among African Americans, Black Caribbeans, and Non-Latino Whites," *Journal of Family Issues* 43, no. 1 (February 19, 2021), https://doi.org/10.1177/0192513X21993188.
39. Peter Kropotkin, *Mutual Aid: A Factor of Evolution* (Heinemann, 1902).
40. Ariel Aberg-Riger, "A Visual History of Mutual Aid," *Bloomberg CityLab*, December 22, 2020, https://www.bloomberg.com/news/features/2020-12-22/a-visual-history-of-mutual-aid?srnd=undefined (accessed September 24, 2024).
41. *Scene on Radio*, "Echoes of a Coup," https://sceneonradio.org/echoes-of-a-coup/ (accessed September 24, 2024).
42. Kimberly Fain, "The Devastation of Black Wall Street," *JSTOR Daily*, July 5, 2017, https://daily.jstor.org/the-devastation-of-black-wall-street/ (accessed October 1, 2024).
43. Heather McGhee, *The Sum of Us: What Racism Costs Everyone and How We Can Prosper Together* (New York: One World, 2021).
44. Ibid., 21.
45. Adedayo Akala, "Cost of Racism: U.S. Economy Lost $16 Trillion Because of Discrimination, Bank Says," NPR, September 23, 2020, https://www.npr.org/sections/live-updates-protests-for-racial-justice/2020/09/23/916022472/cost-of-racism-u-s-economy-lost-16-trillion-because-of-discrimination-bank-says (accessed October 1, 2024).

CHAPTER 2

1. Richard Rothstein, *The Color of Law* (New York: Liveright Publishing, 2017), VII.
2. Ibid., VIII.
3. Sweta Tiwari and Shrinidhi Ambinakudige, "Nearly 1,000 U.S. Streets Named After MLK Jr. What Are They Like?," *HowStuffWorks*, January 10, 2022, https://people.howstuffworks.com/government/local-politics/streets-named-after-mlk.htm (accessed September 24, 2024).
4. Ian Leahy and Yaryna Serkez, "How the U.S. Environmental Movement Overlooked Racism—Until Now," *New York Times*, June 30, 2021, https://www.nytimes.com/interactive/2021/06/30/opinion/environmental-inequity-trees-critical-infrastructure.html (accessed September 24, 2024).
5. Cornell Law School, "Zoning," *Legal Information Institute*, https://www.law.cornell.edu/wex/zoning (accessed September 24, 2024).
6. *Arrested Mobility*, episode 7, "Racialized Zoning," https://arrestedmobility.com/episodes/episode-7-racialized-zoning/ (accessed September 24, 2024).
7. "ZoneCo," https://www.thezoneco.com/ (accessed September 24, 2024).

8. M. Nolan Gray, *Arbitrary Lines: How Zoning Broke the American City and How to Fix It* (New York: Island Press, 2022), 1, Kindle.
9. Ibid., 2.
10. Rothstein, *The Color of Law*, 48.
11. "*Mapping Prejudice Project*," University of Minnesota Libraries, https://mappingprejudice.umn.edu/ (accessed September 24, 2024).
12. *Arrested Mobility*, episode 7, "Racialized Zoning," timestamp 7:00–7:46.
13. Rothstein, *The Color of Law*, 44–45.
14. "Buchanan v. Warley," *Oyez*, https://www.oyez.org/cases/1900-1940/245us60 (accessed September 24, 2024).
15. Kriston Capps, "Buchanan v. Warley: A Housing Milestone at 100," *Bloomberg*, November 5, 2017, https://www.bloomberg.com/news/articles/2017-11-05/-buchanan-v-warley-a-housing-milestone-at-100 (accessed September 24, 2024).
16. Rothstein, *The Color of Law*, 64.
17. Ta-Nehisi Coates, "The Case for Reparations," *The Atlantic*, June 2014, https://www.theatlantic.com/magazine/archive/2014/06/the-case-for-reparations/361631/ (accessed September 24, 2024).
18. "World's Best Jazz Cities," *DownBeat Magazine*, February 2019, https://downbeat.com/digitaledition/2019/DB1902_World%E2%80%99s_Best_Jazz_Cities/_art/DB1902_World%E2%80%99s_Best_Jazz_Cities.pdf (accessed September 24, 2024).
19. Ted Gioia, "How New York City Became the Epicenter of Jazz," *The Observer*, September 26, 2016, https://observer.com/2016/09/how-new-york-city-became-the-epicenter-of-jazz/ (accessed September 24, 2024).
20. National Park Service, "Jazz History and Culture," https://www.nps.gov/jazz/learn/historyculture/jazz-map.htm (accessed September 24, 2024).
21. Digital Scholarship Lab, "Redlining Map of Manhattan," *University of Richmond*, https://dsl.richmond.edu/panorama/redlining/map/NY/Manhattan/area_descriptions/D23#mapview=full&loc=13/40.8177/-73.9059 (accessed September 24, 2024).
22. Digital Scholarship Lab, "Redlining Map of New Orleans," *University of Richmond*, https://dsl.richmond.edu/panorama/redlining/map/LA/NewOrleans/area_descriptions#mapview=full&loc=12/29.99/-90.1045 (accessed September 24, 2024).
23. Digital Scholarship Lab, "Redlining Map of Chicago," *University of Richmond*, https://dsl.richmond.edu/panorama/redlining/map/IL/Chicago/area_descriptions#mapview=full&loc=11/41.7544/-87.6109 (accessed September 24, 2024).
24. Jacqueline Serrato, Charmaine Runes, and Pat Sier, "Mapping Chicago's Racial Segregation," *South Side Weekly*, February 24, 2022, https://southsideweekly.com/mapping-chicagos-racial-segregation/ (accessed September 24, 2024).

25. American Planning Association, "1949 Housing Act," *Planning Magazine*, https://www.planning.org/awards/2014/1949housingact.htm (accessed September 24, 2024).
26. US Department of Transportation, "Federal-Aid Highway Act of 1956."
27. Wendell E. Pritchett, "The 'Public Menace' of Blight: Urban Renewal and the Private Uses of Eminent Domain," *All Faculty Scholarship 1199*, University of Pennsylvania, 2003, https://scholarship.law.upenn.edu/faculty_scholarship/1199 (accessed September 24, 2024).
28. Digital Scholarship Lab, "Urban Renewal Cartogram," *University of Richmond*, https://dsl.richmond.edu/panorama/renewal/#view=/0/0/1&viz=cartogram (accessed September 24, 2024).
29. Digital Scholarship Lab, "Redlining," *University of Richmond*, https://dsl.richmond.edu/panorama/redlining/ (accessed September 24, 2024).
30. "The Story of Redlining and Its Lasting Effects," *YouTube*, https://youtu.be/T8Abhj17kYU (accessed September 24, 2024).
31. Greg Miller, "Urban Renewal Projects Across the United States," *National Geographic*, December 15, 2017, https://www.nationalgeographic.com/history/article/urban-renewal-projects-maps-united-states (accessed September 24, 2024).
32. James Baron, "Lincoln Center and the San Juan Hill Neighborhood," *New York Times*, February 15, 2023, https://www.nytimes.com/2023/02/15/nyregion/lincoln-center-san-juan-hill.html (accessed September 24, 2024).
33. *Arrested Mobility*, episode 6, "Killer Roads," https://arrestedmobility.com/episodes/episode-6-killer-roads/ (accessed September 24, 2024).
34. Smart Growth America, *Dangerous by Design 2022*, https://smartgrowthamerica.org/dangerous-by-design/ (accessed September 24, 2024).
35. Rebecca L. Sanders and Robert J. Schneider, "An Exploration of Pedestrian Fatalities by Race in the U.S.," *Transportation Research Part D: Transport and Environment* 108 (2022), https://doi.org/10.1016/j.trd.2022.103298.
36. *Arrested Mobility*, episode 6, "Killer Roads."
37. *Arrested Mobility*, episode 6, timestamp 18:37–20:13.
38. Elizabeth Evitts Dickinson, "Roland Park Archives: A History of Segregation in Baltimore," *Johns Hopkins University Magazine*, Fall 2014, https://hub.jhu.edu/magazine/2014/fall/roland-park-papers-archives/ (accessed September 24, 2024).
39. Sarah Jacobson, "A Brief History of Housing Segregation in Baltimore," *International Mapping*, October 29, 2021, https://internationalmapping.com/blog/a-brief-history-of-housing-segregation-in-baltimore/ (accessed September 24, 2024).
40. Baltimore City Health Department, *"Neighborhood Health Profile Reports,"* https://health.baltimorecity.gov/neighborhood-health-profile-reports (accessed September 24, 2024).

41. City of Minneapolis, "Neighborhood Demographics Dashboard," https://www.minneapolismn.gov/government/government-data/datasource/neighborhood-demographics-dashboard/ (accessed September 24, 2024).
42. Christian Cardenas, "Minnesota Legal Roadblocks and NIMBYism," *Governing Magazine*, January 23, 2024, https://www.governing.com/urban/minnesota-legal-roadblocks-serve-as-nimbyisms-new-ally (accessed September 24, 2024).
43. Jacquelynn Kerubo, "What Gentrification Means for Black Homeowners," *New York Times*, August 17, 2021, https://www.nytimes.com/2021/08/17/realestate/black-homeowners-gentrification.html (accessed October 3, 2024).
44. Topher Sanders, Kate Rabinowitz, and Benjamin Conarck, "Walking While Black: The Ticketed Feel Targeted," *ProPublica and the Florida Times-Union*, November 16, 2017, https://features.propublica.org/walking-while-black/jacksonville-pedestrian-violations-racial-profiling/ (accessed October 1, 2024).
45. Angie Schmitt, *Right of Way: Race, Class, and the Silent Crisis of Pedestrian Deaths in America* (Washington, DC: Island Press, 2021).
46. *Arrested Mobility*, episode 1, "Jaywalking," timestamp 4:02–4:37, https://arrestedmobility.com/episode-1-jaywalking/ (accessed September 24, 2024).
47. Gersh Kuntzman, "NYPD Targets Blacks and Latinos for Jaywalking Tickets," *Streetsblog NYC*, January 8, 2020, https://nyc.streetsblog.org/2020/01/08/nypd-targets-blacks-and-latinos-for-jaywalking-tickets (accessed September 24, 2024).
48. Charles T. Brown, "*Arrested Mobility Report*," https://arrestedmobility.com/wp-content/uploads/2023/03/Arrested-Mobility-Report_web.pdf (accessed September 24, 2024).
49. *Arrested Mobility*, episode 1, "Jaywalking," timestamp 0:29–0:45.
50. Angie Schmitt, "These Communities Are Making Progress After 'Jaywalking' Reform," https://usa.streetsblog.org/2022/06/23/these-u-s-communities-are-making-safety-progress-after-jaywalking-reform.
51. Kevin Duggan, "Modified 'Jaywalking' Repeal Passes Council," *Streetsblog NYC*, September 26, 2024, https://nyc.streetsblog.org/2024/09/26/modified-jaywalking-repeal-passes-council (accessed December 3, 2024).
52. *Arrested Mobility*, episode 1, "Jaywalking," timestamp 28:33–29:33.
53. *Arrested Mobility*, episode 2, "Sidewalk Riding," timestamp 1:32–2:01, https://arrestedmobility.com/episode-2-sidewalk-riding/ (accessed September 24, 2024).
54. Ibid., timestamp 4:59.
55. Keith Goba, "Six States Consider Legislation to Address Ticket Quotas," *Land Line Media*, February 10, 2024, https://landline.media/six-states-consider-legislation-to-address-ticket-quotas/ (accessed September 24, 2024).
56. Jesus M. Barajas, "Biking Where Black: Connecting Transportation Planning and Infrastructure to Disproportionate Policing," *Transportation Research Part D*, 99 (October 2021), https://doi.org/10.1016/j.trd.2021.103027.

57. Ibid., 7.
58. Ibid., 7.
59. Charles T. Brown, "*Arrested Mobility Report,*" Equitable Cities, March 2023, https://arrestedmobility.com/wp-content/uploads/2023/03/Arrested-Mobility-Report_web.pdf (accessed September 24, 2024).
60. Ibid., timestamp 19:45–20:08.
61. Barajas, "Biking Where Black," 1.
62. Ibid., 1.
63. Charles Brown, Elizabeth Harvey, and James Sinclair, "Barriers to Bicycle Access and Use in Black and Hispanic Communities," 2016, New Jersey Bicycle and Pedestrian Resource Center, https://njbikeped.org/barriers-to-bicycle-access-use-in-black-and-hispanic-communities-2016/ (accessed September 24, 2024).
64. Dan Roe, "Black Cyclists Are Stopped More Often Than Whites, Police Data Shows," *Bicycling*, July 27, 2020, https://www.bicycling.com/culture/a33383540/cycling-while-black-police/ (accessed September 24, 2024).
65. *Arrested Mobility*, episode 2, "Sidewalk Riding," timestamp 29:58–30:46.
66. US Consumer Product Safety Commission, "E-Scooter and E-Bike Injuries Soar: 2022 Injuries Increased Nearly 21%," *CPSC*, 2024, https://www.cpsc.gov/Newsroom/News-Releases/2024/E-Scooter-and-E-Bike-Injuries-Soar-2022-Injuries-Increased-Nearly-21 (accessed September 24, 2024).
67. Aleksandra Bush and Brian Entin, "Shocking Video: 5 Florida Officers Facing Charges After Beating 2 Men During Arrest," *NewsNation*, August 3, 2021, https://www.newsnationnow.com/us-news/south/shocking-video-5-florida-officers-facing-charges-after-beating-2-men-during-arrest/ (accessed September 24, 2024).
68. Rob Hayes, "Beverly Hills: Lawsuit Accuses Police Department of Racially Profiling Black People on Rodeo Drive," ABC7, September 2, 2021, https://abc7.com/beverly-hills-police-racial-profiling-scooter/10993075/ (accessed October 2, 2024).
69. *Arrested Mobility*, episode 3, "Sidewalk Riding II," timestamp 6:25–6:37; 6:49–7:03.
70. Ibid., timestamp 7:31–8:14.
71. Ibid., timestamp 9:29–9:41.
72. Ibid., timestamp 14:46–15:43.
73. American Planning Association, "Ethics Code," *Planning Magazine*, https://www.planning.org/ethics/ethicscode/ (accessed September 24, 2024).
74. "Urban and Regional Planners," Data USA, https://datausa.io/profile/soc/urban-regional-planners (accessed September 24, 2024).
75. Charles T. Brown, "Interviews with Black Scholars in Transportation, Public Health, and Land Use," *Equitable Cities*, September 2021, 23.

76. Veronica O. Davis, *Inclusive Transportation: A Manifesto for Repairing Divided Communities* (Washington, DC: Island Press, 2023), 134, Kindle.
77. *Arrested Mobility*, episode 7, "Racialized Zoning."
78. Smart Growth America, "*Dangerous by Design 2022*," https://smartgrowth america.org/wp-content/uploads/2022/07/Dangerous-By-Design-2022-v3.pdf (accessed September 24, 2024).
79. *Arrested Mobility*, episode 6, "Killer Roads," timestamp 28:31–29:25.
80. City of Minneapolis, "Public Safety Through Environmental Design," https://minneapolis2040.com/policies/public-safety-through-environmental-design/ (accessed September 24, 2024).
81. *National Institute of Crime Prevention*, "Crime Prevention Programs," https://thenicp.com/ (accessed September 24, 2024).
82. Bryan Lee Jr., "How to Design Justice into America's Cities," *Bloomberg*, June 3, 2020, https://www.bloomberg.com/news/articles/2020-06-03/how-to-design-justice-into-america-s-cities (accessed September 24, 2024).
83. Richard A Oppel Jr. and Lazar Gamio, "Minneapolis Police Use of Force Data," *New York Times*, June 3, 2020, https://www.nytimes.com/interactive/2020/06/03/us/minneapolis-police-use-of-force.html?action=click&campaign_id=9&emc=edit_nn_20200603&instance_id=19041&module=Spotlight&nl=the-morning&pgtype=Homepage&regi_id=60538895&segment_id=29949&te=1&user_id=a9792dadd45f48289308f06c3519a324 (accessed September 24, 2024).
84. Marisa DeMull, "It's Time for Transportation Engineers to Address Racial Equity," Alta Planning + Design, *Medium*, August 14, 2020, https://blog.altaplanning.com/its-time-for-transportation-engineers-to-address-racial-equity-edfd183798f6 (accessed September 24, 2024).
85. Marisa Trujillo-DeMull, "The Impacts of Street Lighting on Black and Brown Skin," *LinkedIn*, June 3, 2020, https://www.linkedin.com/pulse/impacts-street-lighting-black-brown-skin-marisa-trujillo-demull-eit/ (accessed September 24, 2024).
86. Lee, "How to Design Justice into America's Cities."
87. Dirk Hoffman, "Beyond the Knife: Social Change in Healthcare," *University at Buffalo*, February 2024, https://medicine.buffalo.edu/news_and_events/news/2024/02/williams-2024-beyond-knife-19025.html (accessed September 24, 2024).

CHAPTER 3

1. Sam Sanders and Kenya Young, "A Black Mother Reflects on Giving Her 3 Sons 'The Talk'—Again and Again," NPR, June 28, 2020, https://www.npr.org/2020

/06/28/882383372/a-black-mother-reflects-on-giving-her-3-sons-the-talk-again-and-again.
2. Ibid.
3. The Stanford Open Policing Project, "Findings," https://openpolicing.stanford.edu/findings/.
4. Drew Desilver, Michael Lipka, and Dahlia Fahmy, "10 Things We Know About Race and Policing in the U.S.," *Pew Research Center*, June 3, 2020, https://www.pewresearch.org/short-reads/2020/06/03/10-things-we-know-about-race-and-policing-in-the-u-s/.
5. New York University, "Black Drivers More Likely to Be Stopped by Police," *NYU News*, May 2020, https://www.nyu.edu/about/news-publications/news/2020/may/black-drivers-more-likely-to-be-stopped-by-police.html.
6. Emma Pierson et al., "A Large-Scale Analysis of Racial Disparities in Police Stops Across the United States," *Nature Human Behaviour* 4, no. 7 (July 2020): 736–45, doi:10.1038/s41562-020-0858-1.
7. Eyder Peralta and Cheryl Corley, "The Driving Life and Death of Philando Castile," *National Public Radio,* July 15, 2016, https://www.npr.org/sections/thetwo-way/2016/07/15/485835272/the-driving-life-and-death-of-philando-castile (accessed September 24, 2024).
8. Ronnie A. Dunn, "Measuring Racial Disparities in Traffic Ticketing Within Large Urban Jurisdictions," *Public Performance & Management Review 32, no. 4, 537–61*, https://www.jstor.org/stable/40586772.
9. "Mapping Police Violence," https://mappingpoliceviolence.us/ (accessed September 24, 2024).
10. Ibid.
11. Stephen Rushin and Griffin Edwards, "An Empirical Assessment of Pretextual Stops and Racial Profiling," *Stanford Law Review* 73, no. 3 (2021): 637.
12. Marin Cogan, "How Cars Fuel Racial Inequality," *Vox*, June 23, 2022, https://www.vox.com/23735896/racism-car-ownership-driving-violence-traffic-violations (accessed September 24, 2024).
13. Ibid.
14. East Bay Community Law Center, "*Stopped, Fined, Arrested: Racial Bias in Policing and Traffic Enforcement in California,*" April 2016, 1, https://ebclc.org/wp-content/uploads/2016/04/Stopped_Fined_Arrested_BOTRCA.pdf (accessed September 24, 2024).
15. Ibid.
16. Peralta and Corley, "The Driving Life and Death of Philando Castile."
17. NYCLU, "Stop-and-Frisk Data," accessed June 27, 2023, https://www.nyclu.org/en/stop-and-frisk-data.
18. "Mapping Police Violence," Mapping Police Violence.org.

19. Ibid.
20. Statista, "Rate of Police Shootings by Ethnicity in the U.S.," https://www.statista.com/statistics/1123070/police-shootings-rate-ethnicity-us/ (accessed September 24, 2024).
21. Pam Johnson, *Justice for Ella: The Story That Needed to Be Told* (iUniverseLLC, 2014), Kindle.
22. Ibid., 227.
23. Gary Potter, "*The History of Policing in the United States*," Eastern Kentucky University, June 25, 2013, https://d1wqtxts1xzle7.cloudfront.net/63685153/the-history-of-policing-in-usa20200619-44096-pw7laa-libre.pdf?1592633095=&response-content-disposition=inline%3B+filename%3DThe_History_of_Policing_in_the_United_St.pdf&Expires=1727895000&Signature=Ez74aXPVX-JQkzpea94cBt-oUOD19EjdxucTohrI1Mj4yud-2xj6X10PQHQ8ClIxBYu0Mgh36yKrbxdCBOXWT4lEddK-h4wvDPm0DUYyC0brPUhxEj3t64AGE1QBc1nu66F0PYs3KceJGpfY4mEs68YLC3aI1hO41ZgQgNfC0HyYLiay5CBnD5cL8DlVcXvP~xq13euuJnTqeED0o9cEjCKT~pY~GmbJ836E626rcCq1BkKGGsUpVb9sf67CpCLeFYL6CDFFi7H3h4SJwlY1uWTjOscZvYVmlDEGXrhiaEy3RTBuoWwnN0GtKp1G0P7j3yElE4AmSJPwAnnb05QLhA__&Key-Pair-Id=APKAJLOHF5GGSLRBV4ZA (accessed September 24, 2024).
24. Ibid., 2.
25. Ibid., 2.
26. National Archives, "The Great Migration," https://www.archives.gov/research/african-americans/migrations/great-migration (accessed September 24, 2024).
27. Potter, "The History of Policing," 3.
28. Ibid.
29. Isabel Wilkerson, *Caste: The Origins of Our Discontents* (New York: Random House, 2020).
30. *PBS News Hour*, "'Caste' Author Isabel Wilkerson on Race Hierarchy," PBS, August 5, 2020, https://www.pbs.org/video/newshour-bookshelf-1596668177/ (accessed September 24, 2024).
31. Charles T. Brown, *Arrested Mobility*, episode 1, "Jaywalking," 11:37–12:17, https://arrestedmobility.com/episode-1-jaywalking/ (accessed September 24, 2024).
32. Juliana Menasce Horowitz, Kiley Hurst, and Dana Braga, "Views of the Treatment of Black People in America," Pew Research Center, June 14, 2023, https://www.pewresearch.org/social-trends/2023/06/14/views-of-the-treatment-of-black-people-in-america/ (accessed October 3, 2024).
33. Potter, "The History of Policing," 13.
34. Charles T. Brown, *Arrested Mobility*, episode 1, "Jaywalking," 10:04–10:13, https://arrestedmobility.com/episode-1-jaywalking/ (accessed September 24, 2024).
35. Ibid., episode 2, "Sidewalk Riding," 20:54–21:40.

36. What Is Vision Zero?" Vision Zero Network, https://visionzeronetwork.org/about/what-is-vision-zero/#:~:text=Vision%20Zero%20is%20a%20strategy,momentum%20in%20major%20American%20cities (accessed September 24, 2024).
37. Kashmir Hill and Ryan Mac, "A Wrongfully Arrested Man Sues Detroit Police for Using Facial Recognition," *New York Times*, March 31, 2023, https://www.nytimes.com/2023/03/31/technology/facial-recognition-false-arrests.html (accessed September 24, 2024).
38. Thaddeus L. Johnson, "Facial Recognition Systems in Policing and Racial Disparities in Arrests," *Government Information Quarterly* 39, no. 4 (October 2022), https://doi.org/10.1016/j.giq.2022.101753.
39. Thaddeus L. Johnson and Natasha N. Johnson, " Police Facial Recognition Technology Can't Tell Black People Apart," *Scientific American*, May 18, 2023, https://www.scientificamerican.com/article/police-facial-recognition-technology-cant-tell-black-people-apart/ (accessed October 1, 2024).
40. Bernard Marr, "The 5 Biggest Tech Trends in Policing and Law Enforcement," *Forbes*, March 8, 2022, https://www.forbes.com/sites/bernardmarr/2022/03/08/the-5-biggest-tech-trends-in-policing-and-law-enforcement/?sh=165360833840 (accessed September 24, 2024).
41. Adrienne So, "Why We Don't Recommend Ring Cameras," *Wired*, July 9, 2023, https://www.wired.com/story/why-we-do-not-recommend-ring/ (accessed December 3, 2024).
42. Ilia Schlitz, "The Bias Inside: A Conversation with Psychologist Jennifer Eberhardt," *Behavioral Scientist*, https://behavioralscientist.org/the-bias-inside-a-conversation-with-psychologist-jennifer-eberhardt/ (accessed September 24, 2024).
43. Ring, "Neighbors Public Safety Service," https://ring.com/neighbors-public-safety-service (accessed October 3, 2024).
44. Dan Calacci, Jeffrey J. Shen, and Alex Pentland, "The Cop in Your Neighbor's Doorbell: Amazon Ring and the Spread of Participatory Mass Surveillance," *Proceedings of the ACM on Human–Computer Interaction* 6, no. CSCW2 (November 11, 2022), https://doi.org/10.1145/3555125.
45. Ibid.
46. Rod McCullom and Undark, "Do Video Doorbells Really Prevent Crime? *Scientific American*, December 14, 2023, https://www.scientificamerican.com/article/do-video-doorbells-really-prevent-crime/ (accessed October 1, 2024).
47. Amanda Geller et al., "Aggressive Policing and the Mental Health of Young Urban Men," *American Journal of Public Health* 104, no. 12 (December 2014): 2321–7, https://doi.org/10.2105/AJPH.2014.302046.
48. Ibid., 2325.

49. From University of California, Riverside, and who was a part of the 2014 Columbia University study.
50. Jordan DeVylder, Lisa Vedina, and Bruce Link, "Impact of Police Violence on Mental Health: A Theoretical Framework," *American Journal of Public Health* 110, no. 11 (November 1, 2020): 1704–10, https://doi.org/10.2105/AJPH.2020.305874.
51. Ibid., 1705.
52. Ashley Nellis, "The Color of Justice: Racial and Ethnic Disparity in State Prisons," The Sentencing Project (August 2022), 13, https://www.sentencingproject.org/app/uploads/2022/08/The-Color-of-Justice-Racial-and-Ethnic-Disparity-in-State-Prisons.

CHAPTER 4

1. Veronica O. Davis, *Inclusive Transportation: A Manifesto for Repairing Divided Communities* (Washington, DC: Island Press, 2023), Kindle.
2. Jordan Levy, "Philly Becomes the First Big U.S. City with a Law Banning Minor Traffic Stops," *Billy Penn at WHYY*, March 3, 2022. https://billypenn.com/2022/03/03/philly-becomes-the-first-big-u-s-city-with-a-law-banning-minor-traffic-stops/ (accessed October 2, 2024).
3. Sammy Caiola, "Data Shows Philly Traffic Stops Involving Black Men Are Down 54%," WHYY, March 6, 2023, https://whyy.org/articles/philadelphia-driving-equality-act-data-traffic-stops-black-men-reduction/ (accessed October 2, 2024).
4. Sam Raim, "Police Are Stopping Fewer Drivers—and It's Increasing Safety," *Vera*, January 11, 2024, https://www.vera.org/news/police-are-stopping-fewer-drivers-and-its-increasing-safety (accessed October 2, 2024).
5. Ibid.
6. Kevin Rector, "New Limits on 'Pretextual Stops' by LAPD Officers Approved, Riling Police Union," *Los Angeles Times*, March 1, 2022, https://www.latimes.com/california/story/2022-03-01/new-limits-on-pretextual-stops-by-lapd-to-take-effect-this-summer-after-training (accessed October 2, 2024).
7. Libor Jany and Ben Poston, "Minor Police Encounters Plummet After LAPD Put Limits on Stopping Drivers and Pedestrians," *Los Angeles Times*, November 14, 2022, https://www.latimes.com/california/story/2022-11-14/minor-traffic-stops-plummet-in-months-after-lapd-policy-change (accessed October 2, 2024).
8. Adam Tuss, "Virginia Decriminalizes Jaywalking," NBC Washington, January 5, 2021, https://www.nbcwashington.com/news/local/transportation/virginia-decriminalizes-jaywalking/2530411/ (accessed September 24, 2024).

9. Angie Schmitt, "Decriminalizing Walking: Notching More Wins," *America Walks Blog*, February 14, 2023, https://americawalks.org/decriminalizing-walking-notching-more-wins/ (accessed September 24, 2024).
10. Ramsey Khalifeh, "'I'm Walking Here': NYC on Track to Legalize Jaywalking," *Gothamist*, September 26, 2024, https://gothamist.com/news/im-walking-here-nyc-on-track-to-legalize-jaywalking (accessed October 2, 2024).
11. National Transportation Safety Board, "Most Wanted List of Transportation Safety Improvements," November 5, 2019, https://www.ntsb.gov/news/press-releases/Pages/NR20191105.aspx (accessed September 24, 2024).
12. David Kroman, "King County Repeals Mandatory Bicycle Helmet Law," *Seattle Times*, February 17, 2022, https://www.seattletimes.com/seattle-news/transportation/king-county-repeals-mandatory-bicycle-helmet-law/ (accessed October 2, 2024).
13. Cortney Sanders and Michael Leachman, "Step One to an Antiracist State Revenue Policy: Eliminate Criminal Justice Fines and Fees," Center on Budget and Policy Priorities, September 17, 2021, https://www.cbpp.org/research/state-budget-and-tax/step-one-to-an-antiracist-state-revenue-policy-eliminate-criminal (accessed September 24, 2024).
14. Davis, *Inclusive Transportation*, 134.
15. *Arrested Mobility*, episode 2, "Sidewalk Riding," 27:27–28:41, https://arrestedmobility.com/episode-2-sidewalk-riding/ (accessed September 24, 2024).
16. George Anders, "Who's Vaulting to the C-Suite? Trends that Changed Fast in 2022," LinkedIn, February 1, 2023, https://www.linkedin.com/pulse/whos-vaulting-c-suite-trends-changed-fast-2022-george-anders/?trackingId=jOiiEvmfQI6sMbG%2BKwpCIQ%3D%3D (accessed September 24, 2024).
17. Reyhan Ayas, Paulina Tilly, and Devan Rawlings, "Cutting Costs at the Expense of Diversity," Revelio Labs, February 7, 2023, https://www.reveliolabs.com/news/social/cutting-costs-at-the-expense-of-diversity/ (accessed September 24, 2024).
18. Southern California Association of Governments, "Regional Early Action Planning (REAP) Final Report," https://scag.ca.gov/sites/main/files/file-attachments/reap_final.pdf?1620325603 (accessed September 24, 2024).
19. Ibid., 9.
20. Ibid., 6.
21. Ibid., 34.
22. Ibid., 29.
23. Southern California Association of Governments, "Resolution No. 20-623-2," https://scag.ca.gov/sites/main/files/file-attachments/rcresolution206232.pdf?1604640361 (accessed September 24, 2024).

24. Southern California Association of Governments, "Special Committee on Equity and Social Justice," https://scag.ca.gov/special-committee-equity-and-social-justice (accessed September 24, 2024).
25. Southern California Association of Governments, "Regional Early Action Planning (REAP) Final Report," 5.
26. Ibid., 3.
27. Ibid., 14.
28. Southern California Association of Governments, "Grant Opportunities," https://scag.ca.gov/get-involved-grant-opportunities (accessed October 2, 2024).
29. Restorative Justice Council, "What Is Restorative Justice?," https://restorativejustice.org.uk/what-restorative-justice (accessed September 24, 2024).
30. Davis, *Inclusive Transportation*, 49.
31. *Arrested Mobility*, episode 1, "Jaywalking," 26:25–27:56, https://arrestedmobility.com/episode-1-jaywalking/ (accessed September 24, 2024).
32. john a. powell, Stephen Mendenian, and Wendy Ake, "Targeted Universalism: Policy & Practice," Othering and Belonging Institute, University of California, Berkeley, https://belonging.berkeley.edu/targeted-universalism (accessed September 24, 2024).
33. US Department of Transportation, "About the Reconnecting Communities Pilot Program," https://www.transportation.gov/grants/rcnprogram/about-rcp (accessed September 24, 2024).
34. Transportation for America, "Reconnecting Communities," August 2, 2022, https://t4america.org/2022/08/02/reconnecting-communities/ (accessed September 24, 2024).
35. US Department of Housing and Urban Development, "Recipient Spotlights: Syracuse," https://www.hudexchange.info/programs/tcta/recipient-spotlights/#Syracuse (accessed September 24, 2024).
36. New York Civil Liberties Union, "The I-81 Story," https://www.nyclu.org/resources/campaigns-actions/campaigns/i-81-story (accessed September 24, 2024).
37. US Department of Transportation, "FY 23 TCP Selected Communities Fact Sheet," April 2024, https://www.transportation.gov/sites/dot.gov/files/2024-04/FY%2023%20TCP_Selected%20Communities%20Fact%20Sheet_v2.pdf (accessed September 24, 2024).
38. US Department of Transportation, "RCP22 Fact Sheets," February 2023, https://www.transportation.gov/sites/dot.gov/files/2023-02/RCP22_Fact_Sheets.pdf (accessed September 24, 2024).
39. ReConnect Rondo, "Our Vision," https://reconnectrondo.com/vision/ (accessed September 24, 2024).

40. ReConnect Rondo, "ULI Report," March 2018, https://reconnectrondo.com/wp-content/uploads/2020/12/ULI-Report-3.2018.pdf (accessed September 24, 2024).
41. Urban Institute, "The Unequal Commute," October 6, 2020, https://www.urban.org/features/unequal-commute (accessed September 24, 2024).
42. Jeff Turrentine, "When Public Transportation Leads to Gentrification," Natural Resources Defense Council, June 1, 2018, https://www.nrdc.org/stories/when-public-transportation-leads-gentrification (accessed September 24, 2024).
43. Oregon Metro, "Get Moving 2020," https://www.oregonmetro.gov/get-moving-2020 (accessed September 24, 2024).
44. You can read more about this project in Lynn Peterson, *Roadways for People: Rethinking Transportation Planning and Engineering* (Washington, DC: Island Press, 2022).
45. City of Portland, "Vision for 82nd," https://www.portland.gov/transportation/planning/82nd-avenue/vision-82nd (accessed October 2, 2024).
46. Isaiah Thompson, "Whatever Happened to Critical Mass?," *Nonprofit Quarterly*, January 23, 2024, https://nonprofitquarterly.org/whatever-happened-to-critical-mass/ (accessed September 24, 2024).
47. Carlos Mejia-Arbelaez et al., "Social Inclusion and Physical Activity in Ciclovía Recreativa Programs in Latin America," *International Journal of Environmental Research and Public Health* 18, no. 2 (January 14, 2021): 655, https://doi.org/10.3390/ijerph18020655.
48. Ibid.
49. Ellie Vorhaben, "Harris Community Action Study Suggests Ciclovía Could Bring Economic, Health, and Social Benefits to Chicago," *Chicago Policy Review*, June 1, 2021, https://chicagopolicyreview.org/2021/06/01/harris-community-action-study-suggests-ciclovia-could-bring-economic-health-social-benefits-to-chicago/ (accessed September 24, 2024).
50. US Department of Transportation, "Promising Practices for Meaningful Public Involvement in Transportation Decision-Making," updated June 25, 2024, https://www.transportation.gov/priorities/equity/promising-practices-meaningful-public-involvement-transportation-decision-making (accessed October 4, 2024).
51. Lynn Peterson, *Roadways for People: Rethinking Transportation Planning and Engineering* (Washington, DC: Island Press, 2022).
52. One that I've referenced here is Veronica O. Davis's book *Inclusive Transportation: A Manifesto for Repairing Divided Communities*, which focuses on community design that is inclusive of diverse experiences where the approach is centered around involving community in the planning process. Another is the community solution-based approach in Lynn Peterson's book, *Roadways for People*. De-

sign as Democracy: Technique for Collective Creativity, edited by David de la Pena, Diane Jones Allen, Randolph T. Hester, Jeffrey Hou, Laura J. Lawson, and Marcia J. McNally, which offers specific ways, activities, and methods to engage community members creatively in the design process. *Anti-Racist Community Engagement: Principles and Practices*, edited by Christina Santana, Roopika Risam, Aldo Garcia-Guevara, Joseph Krupczynski, Cynthia Lynch, John Reiff, Cindy Vincent, and Elaine Ward, offers specific examples of such community engagement based around four principles that go beyond the typical "White savior" approach to community engagement.

53. Asset-Based Community Development Institute, "About," DePaul University, https://resources.depaul.edu/abcd-institute/about/Pages/default.aspx (accessed September 24, 2024).
54. Ibid.
55. The examples of the work in Syracuse and the Urban Land Institute studies of the Rondo neighborhoods, respectively, are examples of this kind of community engagement. They required significant financial investment; they were inclusive to community members, meaning they were held in their neighborhood on their terms and facilitated by people they knew and trusted; and they were open-ended, flexible, and not too rigidly structured within typical planning processes. That is what is needed to truly get to the heart of the needs and solutions for the community.
56. Davis, *Inclusive Transportation*, 71.
57. Ibid., 72.
58. Street Plans Collaborative, "About Tactical Urbanism," *Tactical Urbanism Guide*, https://tacticalurbanismguide.com/about/ (accessed September 24, 2024).
59. John Surico, "It's Been a Deadly Year on U.S. Roads—Except in This City," *Bloomberg*, December 28, 2022, https://www.bloomberg.com/news/features/2022-12-28/it-s-been-a-deadly-year-on-us-roads-except-in-this-city?srnd=citylab&utm_medium=website&utm_source=archdaily.com (accessed September 24, 2024).
60. Street Plans Collaborative, "Urban Design Plans," https://street-plans.com/ (accessed September 24, 2024).
61. Surico, "It's Been a Deadly Year on U.S. Roads—Except in This City."
62. Data USA, "Jersey City, NJ Demographics," https://datausa.io/profile/geo/jersey-city-nj#demographics (accessed September 24, 2024).
63. Office of the Mayor, "Mayor Adams Announces Nearly $30 Million in Federal Funding for Queens Boulevard Safety Improvements," *City of New York*, https://www.nyc.gov/office-of-the-mayor/news/975-23/mayor-adams-nearly-30-million-federal-funding-queens-boulevard-safety-improvements (accessed September 24, 2024).

64. *Arrested Mobility*, episode 2, "Sidewalk Riding," 22:15–40.
65. Jonaki Mehta, "Why Philadelphia Has Banned Low-Level Traffic Stops," *MPR News*, November 8, 2021, https://www.mprnews.org/story/2021/11/08/npr-why-philadelphia-has-banned-low-level-traffic-stops (accessed September 24, 2024).
66. Katie Krzaczek, "Philadelphia Police Won't Stop Drivers for Minor Offenses," *Philadelphia Inquirer*, March 3, 2022, https://www.inquirer.com/news/philadelphia/philadelphia-police-wont-stop-drivers-minor-offenses-20220303.html (accessed September 24, 2024).
67. Anna Orso, Chris Palmer, and Kasturi Pananjad, "Philadelphia Driving Equality Legislation One Year Results," *Philadelphia Inquirer*, March 3, 2023, https://www.inquirer.com/news/philadelphia-driving-equality-legislation-one-year-results-20230303.html (accessed September 24, 2024).
68. Elizabeth Szeto, "City Efforts to Address Racial Bias in Traffic Enforcement Have Reduced the Number of Stops but Disparities Remain," *PublicSource*, July 25, 2023, https://www.publicsource.org/pittsburgh-police-traffic-stop-disparity-accountability-race/ (accessed September 24, 2024).
69. Jordan Blair Woods, "*Traffic Without the Police,*" *Stanford Law Review* 73 (June 30, 2021), https://ssrn.com/abstract=3702680 (accessed September 24, 2024).
70. Ibid., 1476.
71. City of Los Angeles Inter-Departmental Memorandum, "Traffic Alternatives Project Report" (Council File #20-0875), City of Los Angeles, November 30, 2023, https://clkrep.lacity.org/onlinedocs/2020/20-0875_rpt_dot_11-30-23.pdf (accessed October 3, 2024).
72. Nazish Dholakia and Akhi Johnson, "Low-Level Traffic Stops Too Often Turn Deadly. Some Places Are Trying to Change That," *Vera Institute of Justice*, February 9, 2022, https://www.vera.org/news/low-level-traffic-stops-too-often-turn-deadly-some-places-are-trying-to-change-that (accessed September 24, 2024).
73. Woods, "*Traffic Without the Police.*"
74. Ibid., 1508.
75. Ibid., 1489.
76. Ibid., 1488.
77. Ibid., 1479.
78. Doris A. Fuller et al., "Overlooked in the Undercounted: The Role of Mental Illness in Fatal Law Enforcement Encounters," Treatment Advocacy Center, https://www.treatmentadvocacycenter.org/reports_publications/overlooked-in-the-undercounted-the-role-of-mental-illness-in-fatal-law-enforcement-encounters/ (accessed September 24, 2024).
79. Kim Krisberg, "Mental Illness and Fatal Law Enforcement Encounters," *The Nation's Health* 53, no. 9 (2023): 1.2, https://www.thenationshealth.org/content/53/9/1.2 (accessed September 24, 2024).

80. Jackson Beck, Melissa Reuland, and Leah Pople, "Behavioral Health Crisis Alternatives: CAHOOTS," *Vera*, November 2020, https://www.vera.org/behavioral-health-crisis-alternatives/cahoots (accessed September 24, 2024).
81. Ibid.
82. Ilaria Schlitz, "The Bias Inside: A Conversation with Psychologist Jennifer Eberhardt," *Behavioral Scientist*, https://behavioralscientist.org/the-bias-inside-a-conversation-with-psychologist-jennifer-eberhardt/ (accessed September 24, 2024).
83. New Urban Mobility Alliance, https://www.numo.global/ (accessed September 24, 2024).
84. Charles T. Brown, *"Arrested Mobility Report,"* https://arrestedmobility.com/report/ (accessed September 24, 2024).

CHAPTER 5

1. Ta-Nehisi Coates, "The Case for Reparations," *The Atlantic*, June 2014, https://www.theatlantic.com/magazine/archive/2014/06/the-case-for-reparations/361631/ (accessed September 24, 2024).
2. *History.com Editors*, "The Great Migration," *History*, https://www.history.com/topics/black-history/great-migration (accessed September 24, 2024).
3. Digital Scholarship Lab, "Redlining in Chicago," *University of Richmond*, https://dsl.richmond.edu/panorama/redlining/map/IL/Chicago/areas#mapview=full&loc=9/41.8722/-87.803 (accessed September 24, 2024).
4. Tammy Gibson, "MLK's Legacy in North Lawndale, Chicago," *Chicago Defender*, January 17, 2022, https://chicagodefender.com/mlks-legacy-in-north-lawndale-chicago/ (accessed September 24, 2024).
5. Tony Briscoe and Ese Olumhense, "1968 Riots and MLK's Legacy in Chicago," *Chicago Tribune*, August 16, 2018, https://graphics.chicagotribune.com/riots-chicago-1968-mlk/index.html (accessed September 24, 2024).
6. Cook County Treasurer, *"Scavenger Sale Study,"* 2022, https://www.cookcountytreasurer.com/pdfs/scavengersalestudy/2022scavengersalestudy.pdf (accessed September 24, 2024).
7. Chelsie Coren, Kate Lowe, and Jesus M Barajas, "Commuting in Context: A Qualitative Study of Transportation Challenges for Disadvantaged Job Seekers," Redacted Organization, April 2021, https://redactedmagazine.wordpress.com/wp-content/uploads/2021/04/0afd8-commutingincontext-aqualitativestudyoftransportationchallengesfordisadvantagedjob.pdf (accessed September 24, 2024).
8. Ibid., 36.
9. North Lawndale Community Coordinating Council, https://nlcccplanning.org/ (accessed September 24, 2024).

10. Boxing Out Negativity, https://boxingoutnegativity.org/ (accessed September 24, 2024).
11. Coren et al., "Commuting in Context."
12. US Department of Housing and Urban Development, "In-Depth Interview on Interior Challenges," https://www.huduser.gov/portal/rbc/indepth/interior-022822.html (accessed September 24, 2024).
13. Paul Caine, "Proposed Ordinance Aims to Preserve Affordable Housing, Stem Displacement in Chicago's Northwest Side," *WTTW News*, July 11, 2024, https://news.wttw.com/2024/07/11/proposed-ordinance-aims-preserve-affordable-housing-stem-displacement-chicago-s-northwest (accessed September 24, 2024).
14. Mississippi River Commission, "Mississippi River Tributaries Project," *U.S. Army Corps of Engineers*, https://www.mvd.usace.army.mil/About/Mississippi-River-Commission-MRC/Mississippi-River-Tributaries-Project-MR-T/Levee-Systems/ (accessed September 24, 2024).
15. Kenya Ross, "130-Mile Delta Bike Trail Underway," *KNOE*, September 27, 2022, https://www.knoe.com/2022/09/27/130-mile-delta-bike-trail-underway-four-parishes-throughout-nela/ (accessed September 24, 2024).
16. Heart of Louisiana, "St. Joseph, Louisiana: A Town Reborn," https://heartoflouisiana.com/st-joseph-louisiana-rebirth/ (accessed September 24, 2024).
17. World Population Review, "St. Joseph, LA," https://worldpopulationreview.com/us-cities/louisiana/st-joseph (accessed September 24, 2024).
18. Data USA, "Tensas Parish, LA," https://datausa.io/profile/geo/tensas-parish-la#demographics (accessed September 24, 2024).
19. World Population Review, "Lake Providence, LA," https://worldpopulationreview.com/us-cities/louisiana/lake-providence (accessed September 24, 2024).
20. Scenic USA, "Tensas Parish," https://scenicusa.net/050307.html (accessed September 24, 2024).
21. World Population Review, "St. Joseph, LA."
22. Data USA, "Lake Providence Parish, LA," https://datausa.io/profile/geo/lake-providence-la#demographic (accessed October 1, 2024).
23. John D. Sutter, "The Most Unequal Place in America," CNN, October 30, 2013, https://cnn.com/2013/10/29/opinion/sutter-lake-providence-income-inequality/index.html (accessed October 1, 2024).
24. Duke University, "Black Farmers Lost $326B Worth of Land Due to Dispossession and Discriminatory Policies," *Duke University Social Equity Report*, https://socialequity.duke.edu/news/just-about-all-of-our-land-report-shows-black-farmers-lost-326b-worth-of-land-from-dispossession-and-discriminatory-policies/ (accessed September 24, 2024).
25. LSU AgCenter, "Tensas Parish Healthy Communities," https://www.lsuagcenter.com/topics/food_health/healthy-communities/tensas%20healthy%20communities/tensas%20health%20information (accessed September 24, 2024).

26. LSU AgCenter, "East Carroll Healthy Communities," https://www.lsuagcenter.com/topics/food_health/healthy-communities/east-carroll-healthy-communities/health-information (accessed September 24, 2024).
27. Ibid.
28. Ibid.
29. Centers for Disease Control and Prevention, "Why Addressing Social Determinants of Health Is Important," *CDC*, https://www.cdc.gov/about/priorities/why-is-addressing-sdoh-important.html (accessed September 24, 2024).
30. SCAG, "SCAG Go Human Awards Over $460,000 to 16 Community-Based Organizations for Traffic Safety Project," June 6, 2024, https://scag.ca.gov/news/scag-go-human-awards-over-460000-16-community-based-organizations-traffic-safety-projects (accessed October 1, 2024).
31. AIDS LifeCycle, https://www.aidslifecycle.org/ (accessed September 24, 2024).
32. Segregation by Design, "Los Angeles: Sugar Hill," https://www.segregationbydesign.com/los-angeles/sugar-hill (accessed September 24, 2024).
33. Nathan Masters, "Creating the Santa Monica Freeway," PBS SoCal, September 9, 2012, https://www.pbssocal.org/shows/departures/creating-the-santa-monica-freeway (accessed September 24, 2024).
34. Biking While Black, https://www.bikingwhileblack.com/ (accessed September 24, 2024).
35. The community is 68 percent Hispanic/Latino, 14.3 percent Asian, 12.7 percent Black, and 4.2 percent White; Statistical Atlas, "Race and Ethnicity in Arlington Heights, Los Angeles, California," https://statisticalatlas.com/neighborhood/California/Los-Angeles/Arlington-Heights/Race-and-Ethnicity (accessed September 24, 2024).
36. Syracuse University Library, "Intersectionality Research Guide," https://researchguides.library.syr.edu/fys101/intersectionality (accessed September 24, 2024).
37. Julianne Cuba, "Civil Rights Group Calls on High Court to Protect Cyclists' Constitutional Rights," *StreetsblogNYC,* October 17, 2022, https://nyc.streetsblog.org/2022/10/17/civil-rights-group-calls-on-high-court-to-protect-cyclists-constitutional-rights.
38. Patricia Pazner and David L. Goodwin, "Lance Rodriguez Brief," State Court Report, New York, 2021, https://statecourtreport.org/sites/default/files/fastcase/additionalPdfs/processed/Lance%20Rodriguez%20-Brief%20-12.28.2021.pdf (accessed September 24, 2024).
39. Julianne Cuba, "NYPD's Racial Bias in Ticketing Cyclists Continued Last Year," *Streetsblog NYC*, January 4, 2022, https://nyc.streetsblog.org/2022/01/04/nypds-racial-bias-in-ticketing-cyclists-continued-last-year (accessed September 24, 2024).

40. New York Civil Liberties Union, "Stop-and-Frisk Data Report," https://www.nyclu.org/uploads/2019/02/stopandfrisk_briefer_2002-2013_final.pdf (accessed September 24, 2024).
41. Leadership Conference on Civil and Human Rights, "NYPD's Infamous Stop-and-Frisk Policy Found Unconstitutional," *The Leadership Conference*, https://civilrights.org/edfund/resource/nypds-infamous-stop-and-frisk-policy-found-unconstitutional/ (accessed September 24, 2024).
42. This case study was also featured in episode 10 of the *Arrested Mobility* podcast, and many of the quotes and text came from that episode: *Arrested Mobility*, Episode 10, "Reasonable Suspicion: The Case of Lance Rodriguez," https://arrestedmobility.com/episodes/episode-10-reasonable-suspicion-the-case-of-lance-rodriguez/ (accessed September 24, 2024).
43. Mary Wisniewski, "Black Neighborhoods Still See Most Bike Tickets, Police Data Shows," *Chicago Tribune*, February 12, 2018, https://www.chicagotribune.com/2018/02/12/black-neighborhoods-still-see-most-bike-tickets-police-data-show/ (accessed September 24, 2024).
44. Kevin Flores, "Black Cyclists Stopped," The For the Culture Lab, August 10, 2020, https://forthe.org/journalism/black-cyclists-stopped/ (accessed September 24, 2024).
45. Cuba, "NYPD's Racial Bias in Ticketing Cyclists Continued Last Year."
46. Micah Ling, "NYC Cops Can't Pull Cyclists Over Without Probable Cause," *Bicycling*, November 27, 2023, https://www.bicycling.com/news/a45964189/nyc-cops-cant-pull-cyclists-over-without-probable-cause/ (accessed September 24, 2024).
47. New York Civil Liberties Union, "NYCLU Sues Manhattan DA for Records on NYPD Patrolling Private Apartment Buildings," January 23, 2012, https://www.nyclu.org/press-release/nyclu-sues-manhattan-da-records-nypd-patrolling-private-apartment-buildings (accessed September 24, 2024).
48. New York Civil Liberties Union, "Amicus Curiae Brief, People of the State of New York v. Lance Rodriguez," January 23, 2012, https://www.nyclu.org/court-cases/nyclu-amicus-curiae-brief-people-state-ny-v-lance-rodriguez (accessed September 24, 2024).
49. New York Civil Liberties Union, "Ligon v. City of New York: Challenging NYPD's Aggressive Patrolling of Private Apartment Buildings," April 17, 2012, https://www.nyclu.org/court-cases/ligon-v-city-new-york-challenging-nypds-aggressive-patrolling-private-apartment-buildings (accessed September 24, 2024).
50. Ali Bauman, "An Unconstitutional Overreach? CBS2 Investigates NYPD Continuing Banned Practice of Patrolling Private Buildings," CBS News, May 18, 2023, https://www.cbsnews.com/newyork/news/an-unconstitutional-over

reach-cbs2-investigates-nypd-continuing-banned-practice-of-patrolling-private-buildings/ (accessed September 24, 2024).
51. For more on this case and its broader implications, I invite you to listen to the full discussion on my podcast, *Arrested Mobility* (Episode 10: "Reasonable Suspicion: The Case of Lance Rodriguez," https://arrestedmobility.com/episodes/episode-10-reasonable-suspicion-the-case-of-lance-rodriguez/). Additionally, for a comprehensive overview of our findings and recommendations, please refer to the report available at "Arrested Mobility Report."
52. Chelsie Coren et al., "Commuting in Context."
53. Charles Brown et al., "*Barriers to Biking Report*," People for Bikes, https://prismic-io.s3.amazonaws.com/peopleforbikes/6b4cc95b-295d-4947-88fb-839702944c97_PFB-Final-Barriers+to+Biking+REPORT.pdf (accessed September 24, 2024).
54. Susan Blickstein and Charles Brown, "Bicycling Among Black and Latino Women: A 2016 Study," NJ Bike & Pedestrian Resource Center, 2016, https://njbikeped.org/bicycling-among-black-and-latino-women-2016/ (accessed September 24, 2024).
55. Charles Brown, Elizabeth Harvey, and James Sinclair, "Understanding Barriers to Bicycle Access and Use in Black and Hispanic Communities: A 2016 Study," NJ Bike & Pedestrian Resource Center, 2016, https://njbikeped.org/barriers-to-bicycle-access-use-in-black-and-hispanic-communities-2016/ (accessed September 24, 2024).

CONCLUSION

1. Elaine Kamarck and William A. Galston, "Freedom: Harris's Message to America," *Brookings Institution*, August 11, 2021, https://www.brookings.edu/articles/freedom-harriss-message-to-america/ (accessed September 24, 2024).
2. *United Nations*, "Universal Declaration of Human Rights," December 10, 1948, https://www.un.org/en/about-us/universal-declaration-of-human-rights (accessed September 24, 2024).
3. *Human Rights Watch*, "Afghanistan," in *World Report 2023*, https://www.hrw.org/world-report/2023/country-chapters/afghanistan-0#49dda6 (accessed September 24, 2024).
4. Orly Linovski, "Fast Facts: Under-Investment and Over-Policing—Safe Biking for Whom?" *Canadian Centre for Policy Alternatives*, July 15, 2021, https://policyalternatives.ca/publications/commentary/fast-facts-under-investment-and-over-policing-safe-biking-whom (accessed September 24, 2024).
5. Ibid.

6. Mapping Police Violence, "Mapping Police Violence," https://mappingpolice violence.us/?gad_source=1&gclid=Cj0KCQjw9Km3BhDjARIsAGUb4nz0Fd BhAvA-a1s8JhS468T7Wwz516lzw6sFkuWaQJKSSN4ggd-DyQsaAgOz EALw_wcB (accessed September 24, 2024).
7. Southern California Association of Governments, "Regional Early Action Planning (REAP) Final Report," May 2021, https://scag.ca.gov/sites/main/files/file-attachments/reeap_final.pdf?1620325603 (accessed September 24, 2024).
8. Ibid.

BIBLIOGRAPHY

Aberg-Riger, Ariel. "A Visual History of Mutual Aid." *Bloomberg CityLab,* December 22, 2020. https://www.bloomberg.com/news/features/2020-12-22/a-visual-history-of-mutual-aid?srnd=undefined. Accessed September 24, 2024.

AIDS Lifecycle. https://www.aidslifecycle.org/. Accessed September 24, 2024.

Akala, Adedayo. "Cost of Racism: U.S. Economy Lost $16 Trillion Because of Discrimination, Bank Says." *NPR,* September 23, 2020. https://www.npr.org/sections/live-updates-protests-for-racial-justice/2020/09/23/916022472/cost-of-racism-u-s-economy-lost-16-trillion-because-of-discrimination-bank-says. Accessed October 1, 2024.

American Planning Association. "1949 Housing Act." *Planning Magazine.* https://www.planning.org/awards/2014/1949housingact.htm. Accessed September 24, 2024.

American Planning Association. "Ethics Code." *Planning Magazine.* https://www.planning.org/ethics/ethicscode/. Accessed September 24, 2024.

Anders, George. "Who's Vaulting to the C-Suite? Trends That Changed Fast in 2022." *LinkedIn, February 1, 2023.* https://www.linkedin.com/pulse/whos-vaulting-c-suite-trends-changed-fast-2022-george-anders/?trackingId=jOiiEvmfQI6sMbG%2BKwpCIQ%3D%3D. Accessed September 24, 2024.

Aronowitz, Michelle, Edward L. Golding, and Jung Hyun Choi. *The Unequal Costs of Black Homeownership.* Cambridge, MA: MIT Golub Center for Finance and Policy (September 17, 2020). https://mitsloan.mit.edu/centers-initiatives/mit-gcfp/unequal-costs-black-homeownership. Accessed October 2, 2024.

Arrested Mobility. Episode 1, "Jaywalking." https://arrestedmobility.com/episode-1-jaywalking/. Accessed September 24, 2024.

Arrested Mobility. Episode 2, "Sidewalk Riding." https://arrestedmobility.com/episode-2-sidewalk-riding/. Accessed September 24, 2024.

Arrested Mobility. Episode 3, "Sidewalk Riding II." https://arrestedmobility.com/episode-3-sidewalk-riding-ii-micromobility-persons-with-disabilities/. Accessed September 24, 2024.

Arrested Mobility. Episode 6, "Killer Roads." https://arrestedmobility.com/episodes/episode-6-killer-roads/. Accessed September 24, 2024.

Bibliography

Arrested Mobility. Episode 7, "Racialized Zoning." https://arrestedmobility.com/episodes/episode-7-racialized-zoning/. Accessed September 24, 2024.

Arrested Mobility. Episode 10, "Reasonable Suspicion: The Case of Lance Rodriguez." https://arrestedmobility.com/episodes/episode-10-reasonable-suspicion-the-case-of-lance-rodriguez/. Accessed September 24, 2024.

Asset-Based Community Development Institute. "About." *DePaul University.* https://resources.depaul.edu/abcd-institute/about/Pages/default.aspx. Accessed September 24, 2024.

Ayas, Reyhan, Paulina Tilly, and Devan Rawlings. "Cutting Costs at the Expense of Diversity." *Revelio Labs,* February 7, 2023. https://www.reveliolabs.com/news/social/cutting-costs-at-the-expense-of-diversity/. Accessed September 24, 2024.

Baltimore City Health Department. "*Neighborhood Health Profile Reports.*" https://health.baltimorecity.gov/neighborhood-health-profile-reports. Accessed September 24, 2024.

Barajas, Jesus M. "Biking Where Black: Connecting Transportation Planning and Infrastructure to Disproportionate Policing." *Transportation Research Part D* 99 (October 2021). https://doi.org/10.1016/j.trd.2021.103027.

Baron, James. "Lincoln Center and the San Juan Hill Neighborhood." *New York Times,* February 15, 2023. https://www.nytimes.com/2023/02/15/nyregion/lincoln-center-san-juan-hill.html. Accessed September 24, 2024.

Bauman, Ali. "An Unconstitutional Overreach? CBS2 Investigates NYPD Continuing Banned Practice of Patrolling Private Buildings." *CBS News,* May 18, 2023. https://www.cbsnews.com/newyork/news/an-unconstitutional-overreach-cbs2-investigates-nypd-continuing-banned-practice-of-patrolling-private-buildings/. Accessed September 24, 2024.

Beck, Jackson, Melissa Reuland, and Leah Pople. "Behavioral Health Crisis Alternatives: CAHOOTS." *Vera,* November 2020. https://www.vera.org/behavioral-health-crisis-alternatives/cahoots. Accessed September 24, 2024.

BIKETOWN. "Portland's Bike Share Program." https://biketownpdx.com/. Accessed September 24, 2024.

Biking While Black. https://www.bikingwhileblack.com/. Accessed September 24, 2024.

Blickstein, Susan and Charles Brown. "Bicycling Among Black and Latino Women: A 2016 Study." NJ Bike & Pedestrian Resource Center, 2016. https://njbikeped.org/bicycling-among-black-and-latino-women-2016/. Accessed September 24, 2024.

Boxing Out Negativity. https://boxingoutnegativity.org/. Accessed September 24, 2024.

Brancaccio, David, Rose Conlon, and Daniel Shin. "New Research Shows Racial Discrimination in Hiring Is Still Happening at the Earliest Stages." *Marketplace,* August 3, 2021. https://www.marketplace.org/2021/08/03/new-research-shows

-racial-discrimination-in-hiring-is-still-happening-at-the-earliest-stages/. Accessed September 24, 2024.
Briscoe, Tony, and Ese Olumhense. "1968 Riots and MLK's Legacy in Chicago." *Chicago Tribune,* August 16, 2018. https://graphics.chicagotribune.com/riots-chicago-1968-mlk/index.html.
Brown, Charles T. *Arrested Mobility Report.* New Jersey: Equitable Cities, March 2023. https://arrestedmobility.com/wp-content/uploads/2023/03/Arrested-Mobility-Report_web.pdf. Accessed September 24, 2024.
Brown, Charles T. "Interviews with Black Scholars in Transportation, Public Health, and Land Use." *Equitable Cities,* September 2021.
Brown, Charles T. *Arrested Mobility.* Episode 1, "Jaywalking." https://arrestedmobility.com/episode-1-jaywalking/. Accessed September 24, 2024.
Brown, Charles T. *Arrested Mobility.* Episode 2, "Sidewalk Riding." https://arrestedmobility.com/episode-2-sidewalk-riding/. Accessed September 24, 2024.
Brown, Charles T. "*Arrested Mobility Report.*" https://arrestedmobility.com/report/. Accessed September 24, 2024.
Brown, Charles, Susan Blickstein, Slennah Yang, Aashna Jain, and James Sinclair. "*Barriers to Biking Report.*" People for Bikes. https://prismic-io.s3.amazonaws.com/peopleforbikes/6b4cc95b-295d-494. Accessed October 4, 2024.
Brown, Charles T., Devajyoti Deka, Aashna Jain, Anish Grover, and Qingyang Xie. *Bike Share in New Jersey: Where Do We Stand?* Alan M. Voorhees Transportation Center. Rutgers University, February 11, 2020. https://njbikeped.org/wp-content/uploads/2022/09/Bike-Share_02-11-2020_sm.pdf. Accessed September 24, 2024.
Brown, Charles, Elizabeth Harvey, and James Sinclair. "Bicycling Among Black and Latino Women: A 2016 Study." NJ Bike & Pedestrian Resource Center, 2016. https://njbikeped.org/bicycling-among-black-and-latino-women-2016/. Accessed September 24, 2024.
Brown, Charles, Elizabeth Harvey, and James Sinclair. "Understanding Barriers to Bicycle Access and Use in Black and Hispanic Communities: A 2016 Study." NJ Bike & Pedestrian Resource Center, July 2020. https://njbikeped.org/barriers-to-bicycle-access-use-in-black-and-hispanic-communities-2016/. Accessed September 24, 2024.
Brown, Emma. "The Overwhelming Whiteness of U.S. Private Schools." *Washington Post,* March 29, 2016. https://www.washingtonpost.com/news/education/wp/2016/03/29/the-overwhelming-whiteness-of-u-s-private-schools-in-six-maps-and-charts/. Accessed September 24, 2024.
Bush, Aleksandra, and Brian Entin. "Shocking Video: 5 Florida Officers Facing Charges After Beating 2 Men During Arrest." *NewsNation,* August 3, 2021. https://www.cbs17.com/news/south/shocking-video-5-florida-officers-facing-charges-after-beating-2-men-during-arrest/. Accessed September 24, 2024.

Caine, Paul. "Proposed Ordinance Aims to Preserve Affordable Housing, Stem Displacement in Chicago's Northwest Side." WTTW News, July 11, 2024. https://news.wttw.com/2024/07/11/proposed-ordinance-aims-preserve-affordable-housing-stem-displacement-chicago-s-northwest. Accessed September 24, 2024.

Caiola, Sammy. "Data Shows Philly Traffic Stops Involving Black Men Are Down 54%." WHYY, March 6, 2023. https://whyy.org/articles/philadelphiadriving-equality-act-data-traffic-stops-black-men-reduction/. Accessed October 2, 2024.

Calacci, Dan, Jeffrey J. Shen, and Alex Pentland. "The Cop in Your Neighbor's Doorbell: Amazon Ring and the Spread of Participatory Mass Surveillance." *Proceedings of the ACM on Human–Computer Interaction* 6, no. CSCW2 (November 11, 2022). https://doi.org/10.1145/3555125.

California Association of Governments. "Special Committee on Equity and Social Justice." https://scag.ca.gov/special-committee-equity-and-social-justice. Accessed September 24, 2024.

California Health Report. "Black Mothers and Health Disparities." California Health Report, 2018.

Capps, Kriston. "Buchanan v. Warley: A Housing Milestone at 100." Bloomberg, November 5, 2017. https://www.bloomberg.com/news/articles/2017-11-05/-buchanan-v-warley-a-housing-milestone-at-100. Accessed September 24, 2024.

Cardenas, Christian. "Minnesota Legal Roadblocks and NIMBYism." *Governing Magazine*, January 23, 2024. https://www.governing.com/urban/minnesota-legal-roadblocks-serve-as-nimbyisms-new-ally. Accessed September 24, 2024.

Centers for Disease Control and Prevention. *Statistics on Heart Disease Among Black Americans*. Washington, DC: CDC, 2024. https://www.cdc.gov/nchs/fastats/black-health.htm. Accessed September 21, 2024.

Centers for Disease Control and Prevention. "Why Is Addressing Social Determinants of Health Important?" CDC.gov. Last modified October 21, 2021. https://www.cdc.gov/about/priorities/why-is-addressing-sdoh-important.html. Accessed September 24, 2024.

City of Los Angeles Inter-Departmental Memorandum. "Traffic Alternatives Project Report" (Council File #20-0875). City of Los Angeles, November 30, 2023. https://clkrep.lacity.org/onlinedocs/2020/20-0875_rpt_dot_11-30-23.pdf. Accessed October 3, 2024.

City of Minneapolis. "Neighborhood Demographics Dashboard." https://www.minneapolismn.gov/government/government-data/datasource/neighborhood-demographics-dashboard/. Accessed September 24, 2024.

City of Minneapolis. "Public Safety Through Environmental Design." https://minneapolis2040.com/policies/public-safety-through-environmental-design/. Accessed September 24, 2024.

City of Portland. "Vision for 82nd." https://www.portland.gov/transportation/planning/82nd-avenue/vision-82nd. Accessed October 2, 2024.

Coates, Ta-Nehisi. "The Case for Reparations." *The Atlantic*, June 2014. https://www.theatlantic.com/magazine/archive/2014/06/the-case-for-reparations/361631/. Accessed September 24, 2024.

Cogan, Marin. "How Cars Fuel Racial Inequality." *Vox*, June 23, 2022. https://www.vox.com/23735896/racism-car-ownership-driving-violence-traffic-violations. Accessed September 24, 2024.

Cook County Treasurer. "Scavenger Sale Study, 2022." https://www.cookcountytreasurer.com/pdfs/scavengersalestudy/2022scavengersalestudy.pdf. Accessed September 24, 2024.

Coren, Chelsie, Kate Lowe, and Jesus M. Barajas. "Commuting in Context: A Qualitative Study of Transportation Challenges for Disadvantaged Job Seekers." April 2021. https://redactedmagazine.wordpress.com/wp-content/uploads/2021/04/0afd8-commutingincontext-aqualitativestudyoftransportationchallengesfordisadvantagedjob.pdf. Accessed September 24, 2024.

Cornell Law School. "Zoning." Legal Information Institute. https://www.law.cornell.edu/wex/zoning. Accessed September 24, 2024.

Cuba, Julianne. "NYPD's Racial Bias in Ticketing Cyclists Continued Last Year." *Streetsblog NYC*, January 4, 2022. https://nyc.streetsblog.org/2022/01/04/nypds-racial-bias-in-ticketing-cyclists-continued-last-year. Accessed September 24, 2024.

Data USA. "Jersey City, NJ Demographics." https://datausa.io/profile/geo/jersey-city-nj#demographics. Accessed September 24, 2024.

Data USA. "Lake Providence Parish, LA." https://datausa.io/profile/geo/lake-providence-la#demographic. Accessed September 24, 2024.

Data USA. "Tensas Parish, LA." https://datausa.io/profile/geo/tensas-parish-la#demographics. Accessed September 24, 2024.

Data USA. "Urban and Regional Planners." https://datausa.io/profile/soc/urban-regional-planners. Accessed September 24, 2024.

Davis, Veronica O. *Inclusive Transportation: A Manifesto for Repairing Divided Communities*. Washington, DC: Island Press, 2023. Kindle edition.

de Leon, Kristine. "Is Portland Still the Whitest Big City in America?" *The Oregonian/OregonLive*. Last modified October 7, 2022. https://www.oregonlive.com/data/2022/10/is-portland-still-the-whitest-big-city-in-america.html. Accessed September 24, 2024.

DeAngelis, Reed T. "Systemic Racism in Police Killings: New Evidence from the Mapping Police Violence Database, 2013–2021." *Race and Justice* 14, no. 3 (July 2024): 413. https://doi.org/10.1177/21533687211047943. Accessed September 25, 2024.

Del Toro, Juan and Wang, Ming-Te. "Racial Bias in School Discipline: Disparities in Suspensions and Expulsions." *American Psychological Association*, October 7, 2021. https://www.apa.org/news/press/releases/2021/10/black-students-harsh-discipline. Accessed October 4, 2024.

Del Toro, Juan and Wang, Ming-Te. "The Roles of Suspensions for Minor Infractions and School Climate in Predicting Academic Performance Among Adolescents Expulsions." *American Psychologist* 76, no. 3 (2021): 173–85.

DeMull, Marissa, "It's Time for Transportation Engineers to Address Racial Equity." Alta Planning + Design, August 14, 2020. https://blog.altaplanning.com/its-time-for-transportation-engineers-to-address-racial-equity-edfd183798f6. Accessed September 24, 2024.

Desilver, Drew, Michael Lipka, and Dahlia Fahmy. "10 Things We Know About Race and Policing in the U.S." Pew Research Center, June 3, 2020. https://www.pewresearch.org/short-reads/2020/06/03/10-things-we-know-about-race-and-policing-in-the-u-s/. Accessed September 24, 2024.

DeVylder, Jordan, Lisa Vedina, and Bruce Link. "Impact of Police Violence on Mental Health: A Theoretical Framework." *American Journal of Public Health* 110, no. 11 (November 1, 2020): 1704–10. https://doi.org/10.2105/AJPH.2020.305874. Accessed September 24, 2024.

Dholakia, Nazish, and Akhi Johnson. "Low-Level Traffic Stops Too Often Turn Deadly. Some Places Are Trying to Change That." *Vera Institute of Justice,* February 9, 2022. https://www.vera.org/news/low-level-traffic-stops-too-often-turn-deadly-some-places-are-trying-to-change-that. Accessed September 24, 2024.

Dickinson, Elizabeth Evitts. "Roland Park Archives: A History of Segregation in Baltimore." *Johns Hopkins University Magazine,* Fall 2014. https://hub.jhu.edu/magazine/2014/fall/roland-park-papers-archives/. Accessed September 24, 2024.

Digital Scholarship Lab. "Redlining." *University of Richmond.* https://dsl.richmond.edu/panorama/redlining/. Accessed September 24, 2024.

Digital Scholarship Lab. "Redlining in Chicago." *University of Richmond.* https://dsl.richmond.edu/panorama/redlining/map/IL/Chicago/areas#mapview=full&loc=9/41.8722/-87.803. Accessed September 24, 2024.

Digital Scholarship Lab. "Redlining Map of Chicago." *University of Richmond.* https://dsl.richmond.edu/panorama/redlining/map/IL/Chicago/area_descriptions#mapview=full&loc=11/41.7544/-87.6109. Accessed September 24, 2024.

Digital Scholarship Lab. "Redlining Map of Manhattan." *University of Richmond.* https://dsl.richmond.edu/panorama/redlining/map/NY/Manhattan/area_descriptions/D23#mapview=full&loc=13/40.8177/-73.9059. Accessed September 24, 2024.

Digital Scholarship Lab. "Redlining Map of New Orleans." *University of Richmond.* https://dsl.richmond.edu/panorama/redlining/map/LA/NewOrleans/area_de

scriptions#mapview=full&loc=12/29.99/-90.1045. Accessed September 24, 2024.

Digital Scholarship Lab. "Urban Renewal Cartogram." *University of Richmond.* https://dsl.richmond.edu/panorama/renewal/#view=/0/0/1&viz=cartogram. Accessed September 24, 2024.

Duggan, Kevin. "Modified 'Jaywalking' Repeal Passes Council." *Streetsblog NYC.* September 26, 2024. https://nyc.streetsblog.org/2024/09/26/modified-jaywalking-repeal-passes-council. Accessed December 3, 2024.

Duke University. "Black Farmers Lost $326B Worth of Land Due to Dispossession and Discriminatory Policies." Duke University Social Equity Report. https://socialequity.duke.edu/news/just-about-all-of-our-land-report-shows-black-farmers-lost-326b-worth-of-land-from-dispossession-and-discriminatory-policies/. Accessed September 24, 2024.

Dunn, Ronnie A. "Measuring Racial Disparities in Traffic Ticketing Within Large Urban Jurisdictions." *Public Performance & Management Review* 32, no. 4: 537–61. https://www.jstor.org/stable/40586772. Accessed September 24, 2024.

East Bay Community Law Center. *"Stopped, Fined, Arrested: Racial Bias in Policing and Traffic Enforcement in California."* April 2016. https://ebclc.org/wp-content/uploads/2016/04/Stopped_Fined_Arrested_BOTRCA.pdf. Accessed September 24, 2024.

Fain, Kimberly. "The Devastation of Black Wall Street." *JSTOR Daily,* July 5, 2017. https://daily.jstor.org/the-devastation-of-black-wall-street/. Accessed October 1, 2024.

Flores, Kevin. "Black Cyclists Stopped." The For the Culture Lab. https://forthe.org/journalism/black-cyclists-stopped/. Accessed September 24, 2024.

Fowler, Triesta, and Monica Webb Hooper. "It Takes a Village: Community Support and Health Among Black Youth." *Musings from the Mezzanine, National Library of Medicine,* February 23, 2023. https://nlmdirector.nlm.nih.gov/2023/02/23/it-takes-a-village-community-support-and-the-fortification-of-health-among-black-or-african-american-youth/. Accessed September 24, 2024.

Frank Batten School of Leadership and Public Policy. "Batten Expert Chats: 'Racial Bias and Healthcare' with Sophie Trawalter." YouTube, June 24, 2020. https://www.youtube.com/watch?v=1YaHkjNWCjg&list=PLjZn10PE0qnlGbcsNHz9h0AVIYomS30qx&index=14. Accessed September 24, 2024.

Fuller, Doris A., H. Richard Lamb, Michael Biasotti, and John Snook. "Overlooked in the Undercounted: The Role of Mental Illness in Fatal Law Enforcement Encounters." Treatment Advocacy Center, December 2015. https://www.treatmentadvocacycenter.org/reports_publications/overlooked-in-the-undercounted-the-role-of-mental-illness-in-fatal-law-enforcement-encounters/. Accessed September 24, 2024.

Geller, Amanda, Jeffrey Fagan, Tom Tyler, and Bruce G. Link. "Aggressive Policing and the Mental Health of Young Urban Men." *American Journal of Public Health* 104, no. 12 (December 2014): 2321–7. https://doi.org/10.2105/AJPH.2014.302046. Accessed September 24, 2024.

Gersen, Jeannie Suk. "After Affirmative Action Ends." *New Yorker,* June 26, 2023. https://www.newyorker.com/news/daily-comment/after-affirmative-action-ends. Accessed September 24, 2024.

Ghandnoosh, Nazgol and Celeste Berry. "One in Five: Disparities in Crime and Policing." The Sentencing Project, November 2, 2023. https://www.sentencingproject.org/reports/one-in-five-disparities-in-crime-and-policing/. Accessed October 3, 2024.

Gibson, Tammy. "MLK's Legacy in North Lawndale, Chicago." *Chicago Defender,* January 17, 2022. https://chicagodefender.com/mlks-legacy-in-north-lawndale-chicago/. Accessed September 24, 2024.

Gioia, Ted. "How New York City Became the Epicenter of Jazz." *The Observer,* September 26, 2016. https://observer.com/2016/09/how-new-york-city-became-the-epicenter-of-jazz/. Accessed September 24, 2024.

Goba, Keith. "Six States Consider Legislation to Address Ticket Quotas." *Land Line Media,* February 10, 2024. https://landline.media/six-states-consider-legislation-to-address-ticket-quotas/. Accessed September 24, 2024.

Graham, Vince. "Urban Renewal . . . Means Negro Removal." YouTube, June 3, 2015. https://www.youtube.com/watch?v=T8Abhj17kYU. Accessed October 4, 2024.

Gray, M. Nolan. *Arbitrary Lines: How Zoning Broke the American City and How to Fix It.* New York: Island Press, 2022. Kindle edition.

Hanson, Melanie. "Student Loan Debt by Race." *Education Data Initiative.* Last updated May 12, 2024. https://educationdata.org/student-loan-debt-by-race. Accessed September 24, 2024.

Hayes, Rob. "Beverly Hills: Lawsuit Accuses Police Department of Racially Profiling Black People on Rodeo Drive." ABC7, September 2, 2021. https://abc7.com/beverly-hills-police-racial-profiling-scooter/10993075/. Accessed October 2, 2024.

Heart of Louisiana. "St. Joseph, Louisiana: A Town Reborn." https://heartoflouisiana.com/st-joseph-louisiana-rebirth/. Accessed September 24, 2024.

Heitzeg, Nancy A. "'Whiteness,' Criminality, and the Double Standards of Deviance /Social Control." *Contemporary Justice Review* 18, no. 2 (2013): 197–214. https://doi.org/10.1080/10282580.2015.1025630. Accessed September 24, 2024.

Hill, Kashmir, and Ryan Mac. "A Wrongfully Arrested Man Sues Detroit Police for Using Facial Recognition." *New York Times,* March 31, 2023. https://www.nytimes.com/2023/03/31/technology/facial-recognition-false-arrests.html. Accessed September 24, 2024.

History.com Editors. "The Great Migration." *History.* https://www.history.com/topics/black-history/great-migration. Accessed September 24, 2024.

Hoffman, Dirk. "Beyond the Knife: Social Change in Healthcare." *University at Buffalo,* February 26, 2024. https://medicine.buffalo.edu/news_and_events/news/2024/02/williams-2024-beyond-knife-19025.html. Accessed September 24, 2024.

Horowitz, Juliana Menasce, Kiley Hurst, and Dana Braga. "Views of the Treatment of Black People in America." Pew Research Center, June 14, 2023. https://www.pewresearch.org/social-trends/2023/06/14/views-of-the-treatment-of-black-people-in-america/. Accessed October 3, 2024.

Human Rights Watch. "Afghanistan." In *World Report 2023.* https://www.hrw.org/world-report/2023/country-chapters/afghanistan-0#49dda6. Accessed September 24, 2024.

Jackson, Candace. "What Is Redlining?" *New York Times,* August 17, 2021. https://www.nytimes.com/2021/08/17/realestate/what-is-redlining.html. Accessed October 1, 2024.

Jackson, Torsheta. "Private Schools Can Receive Public ARPA Funds." *Mississippi Free Press,* May 2, 2024. https://www.mississippifreepress.org/private-schools-can-receive-public-arpa-funds-mississippi-supreme-court-rules/. Accessed September 24, 2024.

Jacobson, Sarah. "A Brief History of Housing Segregation in Baltimore." *International Mapping,* October 29, 2021. https://internationalmapping.com/blog/a-brief-history-of-housing-segregation-in-baltimore/. Accessed September 24, 2024.

Jany, Libor and Ben Poston. "Minor Police Encounters Plummet After LAPD Put Limits on Stopping Drivers and Pedestrians." *Los Angeles Times,* November 14, 2022. https://www.latimes.com/california/story/2022-11-14/minor-traffic-stops-plummet-in-months-after-lapd-policy-change. Accessed October 2, 2024.

Johnson, Pam. *Justice for Ella: The Story That Needed to Be Told.* iUniverse, 2014. Kindle edition.

Johnson, Thaddeus L. "Facial Recognition Systems in Policing and Racial Disparities in Arrests." *Government Information Quarterly* 39, no. 4 (October 2022). https://doi.org/10.1016/j.giq.2022.101753.

Johnson, Thaddeus L., and Natasha N. Johnson. "Police Facial Recognition Technology Can't Tell Black People Apart." *Scientific American,* May 18, 2023. https://www.scientificamerican.com/article/police-facial-recognition-technology-cant-tell-black-people-apart/. Accessed October 1, 2024.

Kamarck, Elaine and William A. Galston. "Freedom: Harris's Message to America." *Brookings Institution,* August 11, 2021. https://www.brookings.edu/articles/freedom-harriss-message-to-america/. Accessed September 24, 2024.

Kerubo, Jacquelynn. "What Gentrification Means for Black Homeowners." *New York Times,* August 17, 2021. https://www.nytimes.com/2021/08/17/realestate/black-homeowners-gentrification.html. Accessed October 3, 2024.

Khalifeh, Ramsey. "'I'm Walking Here': NYC on Track to Legalize Jaywalking." *Gothamist*, September 26, 2024. https://gothamist.com/news/im-walking-here-nyc-on-track-to-legalize-jaywalking. Accessed October 2, 2024.

Krisberg, Kim. "Mental Illness and Fatal Law Enforcement Encounters." *The Nation's Health* 53, no. 9 (2023): 1.2. https://www.thenationshealth.org/content/53/9/1.2. Accessed September 24, 2024.

Kritz, Fran. "Doctors Often Fail to Listen to Black Mothers, Complicating Births, Survey Finds." *California Health Report*, September 20, 2018, https://www.calhealthreport.org/2018/09/20/doctors-often-fail-listen-black-mothers-complicating-births-survey-finds/ (accessed October 3, 2024).

Kroman, David. "King County Repeals Mandatory Bicycle Helmet Law." *Seattle Times*, February 17, 2022. https://www.seattletimes.com/seattle-news/transportation/king-county-repeals-mandatory-bicycle-helmet-law/. Accessed October 2, 2024.

Kropotkin, Peter. *Mutual Aid: A Factor of Evolution*. Heinemann, 1902.

Krzaczek, Katie. "Philadelphia Police Won't Stop Drivers for Minor Offenses," *Philadelphia Inquirer*, March 3, 2022. https://www.inquirer.com/news/philadelphia/philadelphia-police-wont-stop-drivers-minor-offenses-20220303.html (accessed September 24, 2024).

Kuntzman, Gersh. "NYPD Targets Blacks and Latinos for Jaywalking Tickets." *Streetsblog NYC*, January 8, 2020. https://nyc.streetsblog.org/2020/01/08/nypd-targets-blacks-and-latinos-for-jaywalking-tickets. Accessed September 24, 2024.

Lagomarsino, Valentina. "Racism, Toxic Stress, and Education Policy." *Science in the News*, Harvard Medical School. https://sitn.hms.harvard.edu/flash/2020/racism-toxic-stress-and-education-policy/. Accessed September 24, 2024.

Leadership Conference on Civil and Human Rights. "NYPD's Infamous Stop-and-Frisk Policy Found Unconstitutional." *The Leadership Conference*. https://civilrights.org/edfund/resource/nypds-infamous-stop-and-frisk-policy-found-unconstitutional/.

Leahy, Ian, and Yaryna Serkez. "How the U.S. Environmental Movement Overlooked Racism—Until Now." *New York Times*, June 30, 2021. https://www.nytimes.com/interactive/2021/06/30/opinion/environmental-inequity-trees-critical-infrastructure.html. Accessed September 24, 2024.

Lee, Bryan, Jr. "How to Design Justice into America's Cities." *Bloomberg*, June 3, 2020. https://www.bloomberg.com/news/articles/2020-06-03/how-to-design-justice-into-america-s-cities. Accessed September 24, 2024.

Levinson, Jonathan. "Portland Has 5th Worst Arrest Disparities in the Nation, According to Data." *Oregon Public Broadcasting*. Last modified February 7, 2021. https://www.opb.org/article/2021/02/07/portland-has-5th-worst-arrest-disparities-in-the-nation-according-to-data/.

Bibliography 161

Levy, Jordan. "Philly Becomes the First Big U.S. City with a Law Banning Minor Traffic Stops." *Billy Penn at WHYY,* March 3, 2022. https://billypenn.com/2022/03/03/philly-becomes-the-first-big-u-s-city-with-a-law-banning-minor-traffic-stops/. Accessed October 2, 2024.

Ling, Micah. "NYC Cops Can't Pull Cyclists Over Without Probable Cause." *Bicycling,* November 27, 2023. https://www.bicycling.com/news/a45964189/nyc-cops-cant-pull-cyclists-over-without-probable-cause/. Accessed October 4, 2024.

Linovski, Orly. "Fast Facts: Under-Investment and Over-Policing—Safe Biking for Whom?" *Canadian Centre for Policy Alternatives,* July 15, 2021. https://policyalternatives.ca/publications/commentary/fast-facts-under-investment-and-over-policing-safe-biking-whom. Accessed October 4, 2024.

LSU AgCenter. "East Carroll Healthy Communities." https://www.lsuagcenter.com/topics/food_health/healthy-communities/east-carroll-healthy-communities/health-information. Accessed September 24, 2024.

LSU AgCenter. "Tensas Parish Healthy Communities." https://www.lsuagcenter.com/topics/food_health/healthy-communities/tensas%20healthy%20communities/tensas%20health%20information. Accessed September 24, 2024.

Mandler, C. "Murders of Trans People Nearly Doubled Over Past 4 Years, and Black Trans Women Are Most at Risk, Report Finds." *CBS News,* October 23, 2022. https://www.cbsnews.com/news/transgender-community-murder-rates-everytown-for-gun-safety-report/.

Mapping Police Violence. "Mapping Police Violence." https://mappingpoliceviolence.us/. Accessed September 24, 2024.

Marr, Bernard. "The 5 Biggest Tech Trends in Policing and Law Enforcement." *Forbes,* March 8, 2022. https://www.forbes.com/sites/bernardmarr/2022/03/08/the-5-biggest-tech-trends-in-policing-and-law-enforcement/?sh=165360833840. Accessed September 24, 2024.

Masters, Nathan. "Creating the Santa Monica Freeway." *PBS SoCal,* September 9, 2012. https://www.pbssocal.org/shows/departures/creating-the-santa-monica-freeway.

Maye, Adewale A. "The Myth of Race-Neutral Policy." *Economic Policy Institute,* June 15, 2022. https://www.epi.org/publication/the-myth-of-race-neutral-policy/. Accessed September 24, 2024.

McCullom, Rod, and Undark. "Do Video Doorbells Really Prevent Crime?" *Scientific American,* December 14, 2023. https://www.scientificamerican.com/article/do-video-doorbells-really-prevent-crime/. Accessed October 1, 2024.

McGhee, Heather. *The Sum of Us: What Racism Costs Everyone and How We Can Prosper Together.* New York: One World, 2021.

Mehta, Jonaki. "Why Philadelphia Has Banned Low-Level Traffic Stops." *MPR News,* November 8, 2021. https://www.mprnews.org/story/2021/11/08/npr-why-philadelphia-has-banned-low-level-traffic-stops. Accessed September 24, 2024.

Mejia-Arbelaez, Carlos, Olga L. Sarmiento, Rodrigo Mora Vega, Monica Flores Castillo, Ricardo Truffello, Lina Martinez, Catalina Medina, Oscar Guaje, Jose David Pinzon Ortiz, Andres F. Useche, et al. "Social Inclusion and Physical Activity in Ciclovía Recreativa Programs in Latin America." *International Journal of Environmental Research and Public Health* 18, no. 2 (January 14, 2021): 655. https://doi.org/10.3390/ijerph18020655.

Mele, Christopher. "Army Lifts Ban on Dreadlocks for Black Servicewomen." *New York Times,* February 10, 2017. https://www.nytimes.com/2017/02/10/us/army-ban-on-dreadlocks-black-servicewomen.html. Accessed September 24, 2024.

Miller, Greg. "Maps Show How Tearing Down City Slums Displaced Thousands." *National Geographic,* December 15, 2017. https://www.nationalgeographic.com/history/article/urban-renewal-projects-maps-united-states?loggedin=true&rnd=1699473473817. Accessed September 24, 2024.

Miller, Greg. "Urban Renewal Projects Across the United States." *National Geographic,* December 15, 2017. https://www.nationalgeographic.com/history/article/urban-renewal-projects-maps-united-states. Accessed September 24, 2024.

Mississippi Parents Campaign. "Noxubee County." https://msparentscampaign.org/noxubee-county/. Accessed September 24, 2024.

Mississippi River Commission. "Mississippi River Tributaries Project." *US Army Corps of Engineers.* https://www.mvd.usace.army.mil/About/Mississippi-River-Commission-MRC/Mississippi-River-Tributaries-Project-MR-T/Levee-Systems/. Accessed September 24, 2024.

Morsy, Leila, and Richard Rothstein. *Toxic Stress and Children in Poverty: Causes and Policy Solutions.* Washington, DC: Economic Policy Institute, 2016. https://www.epi.org/publication/toxic-stress-and-childrens-outcomes-african-american-children-growing-up-poor-are-at-greater-risk-of-disrupted-physiological-functioning-and-depressed-academic-achievement/. Accessed September 21, 2024.

National Archives. "The Great Migration." *National Archives.* https://www.archives.gov/research/african-americans/migrations/great-migration. Accessed September 24, 2024.

National Center for Education Statistics (NCES). *"High School Graduation Rates for 2021–2022."* US Department of Education, Institute of Education Sciences. https://nces.ed.gov/programs/coe/indicator/coi. Accessed September 21, 2024.

National Community Reinvestment Coalition. *"Shifting Neighborhoods: Gentrification and Cultural Displacement in Portland, OR."* https://ncrc.org/gentrification-portlandor/. Accessed September 24, 2024.

National Institute of Crime Prevention. "Crime Prevention Programs." https://thenicp.com/. Accessed September 24, 2024.

National Park Service. "Jazz History and Culture." https://www.nps.gov/jazz/learn/historyculture/jazz-map.htm. Accessed September 24, 2024.

National Transportation Safety Board. "Most Wanted List of Transportation Safety Improvements." November 5, 2019. https://www.ntsb.gov/news/press-releases/Pages/NR20191105.aspx. Accessed September 24, 2024.

Nellis, Ashley. "The Color of Justice: Racial and Ethnic Disparity in State Prisons." *Sentencing Project,* October 12, 2021. https://www.sentencingproject.org/reports/the-color-of-justice-racial-and-ethnic-disparity-in-state-prisons-the-sentencing-project/. Accessed September 24, 2024.

New Urban Mobility Alliance. https://www.numo.global/. Accessed September 24, 2024.

New York Civil Liberties Union. "Amicus Curiae Brief, People of the State of New York v. Lance Rodriguez." January 23, 2012. https://www.nyclu.org/court-cases/nyclu-amicus-curiae-brief-people-state-ny-v-lance-rodriguez. Accessed September 24, 2024.

New York Civil Liberties Union. "The I-81 Story," https://www.nyclu.org/resources/campaigns-actions/campaigns/i-81-story. Accessed September 24, 2024.

New York Civil Liberties Union. "Ligon v. City of New York: Challenging NYPD's Aggressive Patrolling of Private Apartment Buildings." April 17, 2012. https://www.nyclu.org/court-cases/ligon-v-city-new-york-challenging-nypds-aggressive-patrolling-private-apartment-buildings. Accessed September 24, 2024.

New York Civil Liberties Union. "NYCLU Sues Manhattan DA for Records on NYPD Patrolling Private Apartment Buildings," January 23, 2012. https://www.nyclu.org/press-release/nyclu-sues-manhattan-da-records-nypd-patrolling-private-apartment-buildings (accessed September 24, 2024).

New York Civil Liberties Union. "Stop-and-Frisk Data Report." https://www.nyclu.org/uploads/2019/02/stopandfrisk_briefer_2002-2013_final.pdf. Accessed September 24, 2024.

New York University. "Black Drivers More Likely to Be Stopped by Police." *NYU News,* May 2020. https://www.nyu.edu/about/news-publications/news/2020/may/black-drivers-more-likely-to-be-stopped-by-police.html. Accessed September 24, 2024.

Nittle, Nadra Kareem. "What Is Internalized Racism?" *ThoughtCo,* March 1, 2021. https://www.thoughtco.com/what-is-internalized-racism-2834958. Accessed September 24, 2024.

North Lawndale Community Coordinating Council. https://nlcccplanning.org/. Accessed September 24, 2024.

Office of the Mayor. "Mayor Adams Announces Nearly $30 Million in Federal Funding for Queens Boulevard Safety Improvements." *City of New York.* https://www.nyc.gov/office-of-the-mayor/news/975-23/mayor-adams-nearly-30-million-fed

eral-funding-queens-boulevard-safety-improvements. Accessed September 24, 2024.

Oppel, Richard A., Jr., and Lazar Gamio. "Minneapolis Police Use of Force Data." *New York Times,* June 3, 2020. https://www.nytimes.com/interactive/2020/06/03/us/minneapolis-police-use-of-force.html. Accessed September 24, 2024.

Oregon Metro. "Get Moving 2020," June 13, 2020. https://www.oregonmetro.gov/get-moving-2020. Accessed September 24, 2024.

Oregon Secretary of State. "*Black in Oregon: A Timeline of Black History.*" Oregon State Archives. https://sos.oregon.gov/archives/exhibits/black-history/Pages/context/chronology.aspx. Accessed September 24, 2024.

Orso, Anna, Chris Palmer, and Kasturi Pananjad. "Philadelphia Driving Equality Legislation One Year Results," *Philadelphia Inquirer,* March 3, 2023. https://www.inquirer.com/news/philadelphia-driving-equality-legislation-one-year-results-20230303.html. Accessed September 24, 2024.

Oyez. "Buchanan v. Warley." https://www.oyez.org/cases/1900-1940/245us60. Accessed September 24, 2024.

Patel, Nikhil Anil, Sina Kianoush, Xiaoming Jia, Vijay Nambi, Stephanie Koh, Jaideep Patel, Anum Saeed, Ahmed Ibrahim Ahmed, Mouaz Al-Mallah, Anandita Agarwala, et al. "Racial/Ethnic Disparities and Determinants of Sufficient Physical Activity Levels." *Kansas Journal of Medicine* 15 (August 2022): 267–72. https://doi.org/10.17161/kjm.vol15.17592.

Pazner, Patricia, and David L. Goodwin. "Lance Rodriguez Brief." State Court Report, New York, 2021. https://statecourtreport.org/sites/default/files/fastcase/additionalPdfs/processed/Lance%20Rodriguez%20-Brief%20-12.28.2021.pdf. Accessed September 24, 2024.

PBS News Hour. "'Caste' Author Isabel Wilkerson on Race Hierarchy." PBS, August 5, 2020. https://www.pbs.org/video/newshour-bookshelf-1596668177/. Accessed September 24, 2024.

Peralta, Eyder, and Cheryl Corley. "The Driving Life and Death of Philando Castile." *National Public Radio,* July 15, 2016. https://www.npr.org/sections/thetwo-way/2016/07/15/485835272/the-driving-life-and-death-of-philando-castile. Accessed September 24, 2024.

Peterson, Lynn. *Roadways for People: Rethinking Transportation Planning and Engineering.* Washington, DC: Island Press, 2022.

Pierson, Emma, Camelia Simoiu, Jan Overgoor, Sam Corbett-Davies, Daniel Jenson, Amy Shoemaker, Vignesh Ramachandran, Phoebe Barghouty, Cheryl Phillipa, Ravi Shroff, and Sharad Goel. "A Large-Scale Analysis of Racial Disparities in Police Stops Across the United States." *Nature Human Behaviour* 4, no. 7 (July 2020): 736–45. https://doi.org/10.1038/s41562-020-0858-1.

Police Violence Report. "Documenting Police Violence in the United States." https://policeviolencereport.org. Accessed September 24, 2024.

Bibliography

Portland Bureau of Transportation. "High Crash Network Streets and Intersections." Portland.gov. https://www.portland.gov/transportation/vision-zero/high-crash-network-streets-and-intersections Accessed September 24, 2024.

Potter, Gary. "*The History of Policing in the United States,*" Eastern Kentucky University, June 25, 2013.

Powell, John a., Stephen Mendenian, and Wendy Ake, "Targeted Universalism." *University of California, Berkeley.* https://belonging.berkeley.edu/targeted-universalism. Accessed September 24, 2024.

Pritchett, Wendell E. "The 'Public Menace' of Blight: Urban Renewal and the Private Uses of Eminent Domain." *All Faculty Scholarship* 1199, *University of Pennsylvania,* 2003. https://scholarship.law.upenn.edu/faculty_scholarship/1199. Accessed September 24, 2024.

Raifman, Matthew A. and Ernani F. Choma. "Study on Black Americans' Mortality Rates per Mile of Travel," Boston University School of Public Health and Harvard T.H. Chan School of Public Health, 2022.

Raim, Sam. "Police Are Stopping Fewer Drivers—and It's Increasing Safety." *Vera,* January 11, 2024. https://www.vera.org/news/police-are-stopping-fewer-drivers-and-its-increasing-safety. Accessed October 2, 2024.

Ray, Rashawn, Andre M. Perry, David Harshbarger, Samantha Elizondo, and Alexandra Gibbons. "Homeownership, Racial Segregation, and Policies for Racial Wealth Equity." *Brookings,* September 1, 2021. https://www.brookings.edu/articles/homeownership-racial-segregation-and-policies-for-racial-wealth-equity/. Accessed September 24, 2024.

ReConnect Rondo. "Our Vision." https://reconnectrondo.com/vision/. Accessed September 24, 2024.

ReConnect Rondo. "ULI Report," March 2018. https://reconnectrondo.com/wp-content/uploads/2020/12/ULI-Report-3.2018.pdf. Accessed September 24, 2024.

Rector, Kevin. "New Limits on 'Pretextual Stops' by LAPD Officers Approved, Riling Police Union." *Los Angeles Times,* March 1, 2022. https://www.latimes.com/california/story/2022-03-01/new-limits-on-pretextual-stops-by-lapd-to-take-effect-this-summer-after-training. Accessed October 2, 2024.

Restorative Justice Council. "What Is Restorative Justice?" https://restorativejustice.org.uk/what-restorative-justice. Accessed September 24, 2024.

Reynolds, Liam, Vanessa G. Perry, and Jung Hyun Choi. "Closing the Homeownership Gap Will Require Rooting Systemic Racism Out of Mortgage Underwriting." Urban Institute, October 12, 2021. https://www.urban.org/urban-wire/closing-homeownership-gap-will-require-rooting-systemic-racism-out-mortgage-underwriting. Accessed September 24, 2024.

Ring. "Neighbors Public Safety Service." https://ring.com/neighbors-public-safety-service. Accessed October 3, 2024.

Roe, Dan. "Black Cyclists Are Stopped More Often Than Whites, Police Data Shows." *Bicycling*, July 27, 2020. https://www.bicycling.com/culture/a33383540/cycling-while-black-police/. Accessed September 24, 2024.

Ross, Kenya. "130-Mile Delta Bike Trail Underway." KNOE, September 27, 2022. https://www.knoe.com/2022/09/27/130-mile-delta-bike-trail-underway-four-parishes-throughout-nela/.

Rothstein, Richard. *The Color of Law: A Forgotten History of How Our Government Segregated America*. New York: Liveright, 2017.

Rushin, Stephen, and Griffin Edwards. "An Empirical Assessment of Pretextual Stops and Racial Profiling." *Stanford Law Review* 73, no. 3 (2021): 637.

Sanders, Cortney, and Michael Leachman. "Step One to an Antiracist State Revenue Policy: Eliminate Criminal Justice Fines and Fees." Center on Budget and Policy Priorities, September 17, 2021. https://www.cbpp.org/research/state-budget-and-tax/step-one-to-an-antiracist-state-revenue-policy-eliminate-criminal. Accessed September 24, 2024.

Sanders, Rebecca L., and Robert J. Schneider. "An Exploration of Pedestrian Fatalities by Race in the U.S." *Transportation Research Part D: Transport and Environment* 108 (2022). https://doi.org/10.1016/j.trd.2022.103298.

Sanders, Sam, and Kenya Young. "A Black Mother Reflects on Giving Her 3 Sons 'The Talk'—Again and Again." NPR, June 28, 2020. https://www.npr.org/2020/06/28/882383372/a-black-mother-reflects-on-giving-her-3-sons-the-talk-again-and-again. Accessed September 24, 2024.

Sanders, Topher, Kate Rabinowitz, and Benjamin Conarck. "Walking While Black: The Ticketed Feel Targeted." ProPublica and *Florida Times-Union*, November 16, 2017. https://features.propublica.org/walking-while-black/jacksonville-pedestrian-violations-racial-profiling/. Accessed October 1, 2024.

Scene on Radio. "Echoes of a Coup." https://sceneonradio.org/echoes-of-a-coup/. Accessed September 24, 2024.

Scenic USA. "Tensas Parish." https://scenicusa.net/050307.html. Accessed September 24, 2024.

Schlitz, Ilaria. "The Bias Inside: A Conversation with Psychologist Jennifer Eberhardt." *Behavioral Scientist*, May 29, 2019. https://behavioralscientist.org/the-bias-inside-a-conversation-with-psychologist-jennifer-eberhardt/. Accessed September 24, 2024.

Schmidt, Logan, Micah Haskell-Hoehl, and Hayne Yoon. "Target 2020: Police Violence by the Numbers." *Vera*, July 7, 2020. https://www.vera.org/news/target-2020/data-backed-outrage-police-violence-by-the-numbers. Accessed September 24, 2024.

Schmitt, Angie. "Decriminalizing Walking: Notching More Wins." *America Walks Blog*, February 14, 2023. https://americawalks.org/decriminalizing-walking-notching-more-wins/. Accessed September 24, 2024.

Schmitt, Angie. *Right of Way: Race, Class, and the Silent Crisis of Pedestrian Deaths in America*. Washington, DC: Island Press, 2021.

Schmitt, Angie. "These U.S. Communities Are Making Safety Progress After Jaywalking Reform." *Streetsblog USA*, June 23, 2022. https://usa.streetsblog.org/2022/06/23/these-u-s-communities-are-making-safety-progress-after-jaywalking-reform/. Accessed September 24, 2024.

Segregation by Design. "Los Angeles: Sugar Hill." https://www.segregationbydesign.com/los-angeles/sugar-hill. Accessed September 24, 2024.

Seo, Sarah. *Policing the Open Road: How Cars Transformed American Freedom*. Cambridge, MA: Harvard University Press, 2019.

Seratto, Jacqueline, Charmaine Runes, and Pat Sier. "Mapping Chicago's Racial Segregation." *South Side Weekly, February 24, 2022*. https://southsideweekly.com/mapping-chicagos-racial-segregation/. Accessed September 24, 2024.

Smart Growth America. *Dangerous by Design 2022*. https://smartgrowthamerica.org/wp-content/uploads/2022/07/Dangerous-By-Design-2022-v3.pdf. Accessed September 24, 2024.

So, Adrienne. "Why We Don't Recommend Ring Cameras." *Wired*, July 9, 2023. https://www.wired.com/story/why-we-do-not-recommend-ring/. Accessed December 3, 2024.

Southern California Association of Governments. "Grant Opportunities." https://scag.ca.gov/get-involved-grant-opportunities. Accessed October 2, 2024.

Southern California Association of Governments. "Regional Early Action Planning (REAP) Final Report," May 2021. https://scag.ca.gov/sites/main/files/file-attachments/reeap_final.pdf?1620325603. Accessed September 24, 2024.

Southern California Association of Governments. "Resolution No. 20-623-2." https://scag.ca.gov/sites/main/files/file-attachments/rcresolution206232.pdf?1604640361. Accessed September 24, 2024.

Southern California Association of Governments. "SCAG Go Human Awards Over $460,000 to 16 Community-Based Organizations for Traffic Safety Projects." June 6, 2024. https://scag.ca.gov/news/scag-go-human-awards-over-460000-16-community-based-organizations-traffic-safety-projects.

Stanford Open Policing Project. "Findings on Racial Disparities." https://openpolicing.stanford.edu/findings/. Accessed September 24, 2024.

Statista. "Rate of Police Shootings by Ethnicity in the U.S." https://www.statista.com/statistics/1123070/police-shootings-rate-ethnicity-us/. Accessed September 24, 2024.

Statistical Atlas. "Race and Ethnicity in Arlington Heights, Los Angeles, California." https://statisticalatlas.com/neighborhood/California/Los-Angeles/Arlington-Heights/Race-and-Ethnicity. Accessed September 24, 2024.

Street Plans Collaborative. https://street-plans.com/. Accessed September 24, 2024.

Street Plans Collaborative. "About Tactical Urbanism." *Tactical Urbanism Guide*. https://tacticalurbanismguide.com/about/. Accessed September 24, 2024.

Surico, John. "It's Been a Deadly Year on U.S. Roads—Except in This City." Bloomberg, December 28, 2022. https://www.bloomberg.com/news/features/2022-12-28/it-s-been-a-deadly-year-on-us-roads-except-in-this-city?srnd=citylab&utm_medium=website&utm_source=archdaily.com. Accessed September 24, 2024.

Sutter, John D. "The Most Unequal Place in America." CNN, October 30, 2013. https://cnn.com/2013/10/29/opinion/sutter-lake-providence-income-inequality/index.html. Accessed October 1, 2024.

Syracuse University Library. "Intersectionality Research Guide." https://researchguides.library.syr.edu/fys101/intersectionality. Accessed September 24, 2024.

Szeto, Elizabeth. "City Efforts to Address Racial Bias in Traffic Enforcement Have Reduced the Number of Stops but Disparities Remain." PublicSource, July 25, 2023. https://www.publicsource.org/pittsburgh-police-traffic-stop-disparity-accountability-race/. Accessed September 24, 2024.

Tatum, Beverly Daniel. *Why Are All the Black Kids Sitting Together in the Cafeteria? And Other Conversations About Race*. Twentieth Anniversary ed. New York: Basic Books, 2017.

Taylor, Robert, Linda Chatters, Christina J. Cross, and Dawne Mouzon, "Fictive Kin Networks Among African Americans, Black Caribbeans, and Non-Latino Whites." *Journal of Family Issues* 43, no. 1 (February 19, 2021). https://doi.org/10.1177/0192513X21993188.

Templeton, Amelia. "Earlier Releases Surface for Man Charged with Stabbing Black Teens on Portland MAX Train." *OPB*, September 12, 2023. https://www.opb.org/article/2023/09/12/earlier-releases-man-charged-with-stabbing-black-teens-portland-max-train/. Accessed October 4, 2024.

Thompson, Isaiah. "Whatever Happened to Critical Mass?" *Nonprofit Quarterly*, January 23, 2024. https://nonprofitquarterly.org/whatever-happened-to-critical-mass/. Accessed September 24, 2024.

Tiwari, Sweta, and Shrinidhi Ambinakudige. "Nearly 1,000 U.S. Streets Named After MLK Jr. What Are They Like?" *HowStuffWorks*, January 10, 2022. https://people.howstuffworks.com/government/local-politics/streets-named-after-mlk.htm. Accessed September 24, 2024.

Transportation for America. "Reconnecting Communities." August 2, 2022. https://t4america.org/2022/08/02/reconnecting-communities/. Accessed September 24, 2024.

Trujillo-DeMull, Marisa. "The Impacts of Street Lighting on Black and Brown Skin." LinkedIn, June 3, 2020. https://www.linkedin.com/pulse/impacts-street-lighting-black-brown-skin-marisa-trujillo-demull-eit/. Accessed September 24, 2024.

Turrentine, Jeff. "When Public Transportation Leads to Gentrification." Natural Resources Defense Council, June 1, 2018. https://www.nrdc.org/stories/when-public-transportation-leads-gentrification. Accessed September 24, 2024.

Tuss, Adam. "Virginia Decriminalizes Jaywalking." NBC Washington, January 5, 2021. https://www.nbcwashington.com/news/local/transportation/virginia-decriminalizes-jaywalking/2530411/. Accessed September 24, 2024.

United Nations. "Universal Declaration of Human Rights." United Nations, December 10, 1948. https://www.un.org/en/about-us/universal-declaration-of-human-rights.

University of Minnesota Libraries, "Mapping Prejudice Project." https://mappingprejudice.umn.edu/. Accessed September 24, 2024.

Urban Institute. "The Unequal Commute." https://www.urban.org/features/unequal-commute. Accessed September 24, 2024.

US Bureau of Labor Statistics. "Unemployment Statistics by Race (2023–2024)." https://www.bls.gov/web/empsit/cpsee_e16.htm. Accessed September 21, 2024.

US Consumer Product Safety Commission. "E-Scooter and E-Bike Injuries Soar: 2022 Injuries Increased Nearly 21%." CPSC, 2024. https://www.cpsc.gov/Newsroom/News-Releases/2024/E-Scooter-and-E-Bike-Injuries-Soar-2022-Injuries-Increased-Nearly-21. Accessed September 24, 2024.

US Department of Housing and Urban Development. "In-Depth Interview on Interior Challenges." https://www.huduser.gov/portal/rbc/indepth/interior-022822.html. Accessed September 24, 2024.

US Department of Housing and Urban Development. "Recipient Spotlights: Syracuse." https://www.hudexchange.info/programs/tcta/recipient-spotlights/#Syracuse. Accessed September 24, 2024.

US Department of Transportation. "About the Reconnecting Communities Pilot Program." https://www.transportation.gov/grants/rcnprogram/about-rcp. Accessed September 24, 2024.

US Department of Transportation. "Federal-Aid Highway Act of 1956: Creating the Interstate System." *Public Roads Magazine*, Summer 1996. https://highways.dot.gov/public-roads/summer-1996/federal-aid-highway-act-1956-creating-interstate-system. Accessed September 24, 2024.

US Department of Transportation. "FY 23 TCP Selected Communities Fact Sheet." April 2024. https://www.transportation.gov/sites/dot.gov/files/2024-04/FY%2023%20TCP_Selected%20Communities%20Fact%20Sheet_v2.pdf. Accessed September 24, 2024.

US Department of Transportation. "Promising Practices for Meaningful Public Involvement in Transportation Decision-Making," updated June 25, 2024. https://www.transportation.gov/priorities/equity/promising-practices-meaningful-public-involvement-transportation-decision-making (accessed October 4, 2024).

US Department of Transportation. "RCP22 Fact Sheets." February 2023. https://www.transportation.gov/sites/dot.gov/files/2023-02/RCP22_Fact_Sheets.pdf. Accessed September 24, 2024.

Vision Zero Network. "What Is Vision Zero?" https://visionzeronetwork.org/about/what-is-vision-zero/#:~:text=Vision%20Zero%20is%20a%20strategy,momentum%20in%20major%20American%20cities. Accessed September 24, 2024.

Vorhaben, Ellie. "Harris Community Action Study Suggests Ciclovía Could Bring Economic, Health, and Social Benefits to Chicago." *Chicago Policy Review*, June 1, 2021. https://chicagopolicyreview.org/2021/06/01/harris-community-action-study-suggests-ciclovia-could-bring-economic-health-social-benefits-to-chicago/. Accessed September 24, 2024.

White, Gillian B. "Why Black Workers Really Do Need to Be Twice as Good." *The Atlantic*, October 7, 2015, https://www.theatlantic.com/business/archive/2015/10/why-black-workers-really-do-need-to-be-twice-as-good/409276/. Accessed October 4, 2024.

White House, The. "Justice 40 Initiative." https://www.whitehouse.gov/environmentaljustice/justice40/. Accessed October 3, 2024.

Wilkerson, Isabel. *Caste: The Origins of Our Discontents*. New York: Random House, 2020.

Williams, Serena. "What My Life-Threatening Experience Taught Me About Giving Birth." CNN, February 20, 2018. https://www.cnn.com/2018/02/20/opinions/protect-mother-pregnancy-williams-opinion/index.html. Accessed October 3, 2024.

Wilson, Conrad. "Jeremy Christian Sentenced to 2 Life Terms in Prison for 2017 MAX Stabbings." *OPB*, last modified June 24, 2020. https://www.opb.org/news/article/jeremy-christian-sentencing-hearing-victim-impact-statements-portland-oregon/. Accessed October 4, 2024.

Winship, Scott, Christopher Pulliam, Ariel Gelrud Shiro, Richard V. Reeves, and Santiago Deambrosi. "Long Shadows: The Black–White Gap in Multigenerational Poverty." Brookings, June 10, 2021. Accessed September 24, 2024. https://www.brookings.edu/articles/long-shadows-the-black-white-gap-in-multigenerational-poverty/

Wisniewski, Mary. "Black Neighborhoods Still See Most Bike Tickets, Police Data Shows." *Chicago Tribune*, February 12, 2018. https://www.chicagotribune.com/2018/02/12/black-neighborhoods-still-see-most-bike-tickets-police-data-show/.

Woods, Jordan Blair. "Traffic Without the Police." *Stanford Law Review* 73 (June 30, 2021). Accessed September 24, 2024. https://ssrn.com/abstract=3702680.

World Population Review. "Lake Providence, LA." https://worldpopulationreview.com/us-cities/louisiana/lake-providence. Accessed September 24, 2024.

World Population Review. "St. Joseph, LA." https://worldpopulationreview.com/us-cities/louisiana/st-joseph. Accessed September 24, 2024.

"World's Best Jazz Cities." *DownBeat Magazine,* February 2019. https://downbeat.com/digitaledition/2019/DB1902_World%E2%80%99s_Best_Jazz_Cities/_art/DB1902_World%E2%80%99s_Best_Jazz_Cities.pdf. Accessed September 24, 2024.

The Zoning Company. https://www.thezoneco.com/. Accessed September 24, 2024.

ABOUT THE AUTHOR

Charles T. Brown is a trailblazing expert and global authority on urban planning and transportation equity. As the founder and CEO of Equitable Cities, he has redefined how governments worldwide approach mobility, health, and justice. Appointed by US Secretary of Transportation Pete Buttigieg to the Advisory Committee on Transportation Equity and the EV Working Group, formed by the Joint Office of Energy and Transportation, Charles influences national policy at the highest levels. He is a recipient of the National Highway Traffic Safety Administration Public Service Award and a military veteran honored with the Mississippi Commendation Medal and Global War on Terrorism Service Medal. Charles's journey from Shuqualak, Mississippi, to global leadership is a testament to his relentless commitment to transforming communities.